IEO

OLYMPIAD WORKBOOK

INTERNATIONAL ENGLISH OLYMPIAD

01 Learning Objectives

02 Multiple Choice Questions

03 HOTS (Achievers Section)

04 Model Test Paper

05 Answer Keys and Solutions

06 OMR Answer Sheet

V&S PUBLISHERS

Published by:

V&S PUBLISHERS

F-2/16, Ansari road, Daryaganj, New Delhi-110002
☎ 23240026, 23240027 • *Fax:* 011-23240028
✉ info@vspublishers.com • ⊕ www.vspublishers.com

Online Brandstore: amazon.in/vspublishers

Regional Office : Hyderabad
5-1-707/1, Brij Bhawan (Beside Central Bank of India Lane)
Bank Street, Koti, Hyderabad - 500 095
☎ 040-24737290
✉ vspublishershyd@gmail.com

Follow us on:   

BUY OUR BOOKS FROM: | AMAZON | | FLIPKART |

© **Copyright:** *V&S* PUBLISHERS
ISBN 978-81-978021-1-9
New Edition

PUBLISHER'S NOTE

V&S Publishers has carved a significant niche in the publishing industry over the last decade, having successfully published more than 1000 titles across 9 languages spanning over 50 subject categories. Being known for the quality of content, we have built a reputation of excellence and reliability. We have consistently delivered **"Value & Substance"** to our readers, through a wide range of titles across a variety of genres covering school books, fiction and non-fiction that caters to different people from every section of the society.

The **Olympiad Guidebooks for classes 1-10** across all subjects, launched almost a decade ago, under the **GEN X Imprint**, became a go-to-source for the school students in no time, owing to their invaluable and substantive content written in a guidebook pattern,.

Having successfully sold a million copies of the same and in response to demand by both students as well as shopkeepers nationwide; we now present before you our newly launched **Olympiad Workbook Series**, designed for **classes 1-10 across 4 subjects**.

The workbooks are meticulously curated by a team of experienced educators, researchers and subject matter experts, edited by professionals and peer reviewed by teachers. The team has poured its efforts and expertise into creating a crisp and concise workbook which will help and guide the students to the path of success in Olympiad exams. The **MCQs** identified will not only help in scoring top marks in Olympiads but also inculcate a sense of deeper understanding of the subject, by way of solving **HOTS** and referring to complete solutions at the end of the book.

Here we present our new release– **OLYMPIAD WORKBOOK (IEO) CLASS-7** having following features:

☞ Based on the latest syllabi

☞ MCQs with comprehensive coverage of topics

☞ HOTS Questions liberally included

☞ A dedicated chapter on logical reasoning

☞ Model test paper for thorough practice

☞ Sample OMR sheet for real time simulation

We have made sure through our best efforts, that this workbook strictly follows the latest syllabi and patterns of the Olympiad Examination.

As **V&S Publishers** continuously strive to enhance the readability and maintain the credibility of our academic publications, we seek the support of our valuable readers in influencing and enriching the lives of future generations of students.

P.S. While every care has been taken to ensure the correctness of the content, if you come across any error, howsoever minor, do not hesitate to discuss with teachers while pointing that out to us in no uncertain terms.

We wish you all the best for your exams!

DISTINCTIVE FEATURES

01 Learning Objectives

They list the whole chapter as subtopics, helping the teachers to guide children in a step-by-step manner.

02 Multiple Choice Questions

MCQs act as an excellent learning aid, helping you to understand and work on your mistakes.

03 HOTS (Achievers Section)

The High Order Thinking Questions aim to help the student to solve Application-based questions and gain practical understanding of the subject.

04 Model Test Paper

Model test paper are provided at the end of each book, which help the student to test the knowledge which they have gained after thorough reading of all chapters.

05 Answer Key

Detailed Answer Key along with explanations aid the pupil to indentify, understand the mistakes they make during the course of Olympiad preparation.

CONTENTS

SYNONYMS, ANTONYMS, HOMONYMS AND HOMOPHONES

LEARNING OBJECTIVES

➤ Some common Synonyms and Antonyms
➤ Some common Homonyms and Homophones

PRACTICE EXERCISE

I. Choose the correct synonym for the given word.

1. Kind
   (A) nice   (B) wild
   (C) funny   (D) best

2. Glad
   (A) broken   (B) happy
   (C) open   (D) round

3. Fast
   (A) clear   (B) main
   (C) clean   (D) quick

4. Shiny
   (A) extra   (B) careful
   (C) bright   (D) angry

5. Big
   (A) large   (B) many
   (C) next   (D) only

6. Noisy
   (A) first   (B) loud
   (C) afraid   (D) small

7. Final
   (A) last   (B) first
   (C) heavy   (D) small

8. Tired
   (A) kind   (B) fatigued
   (C) ready   (D) angry

9. Merry
   (A) safe   (B) happy
   (C) upset   (D) angry

10. Unhappy
    (A) playful   (B) alive
    (C) sad   (D) angry

11. Similar
    (A) correct   (B) different
    (C) alike   (D) unequal

12. Smart
    (A) dumb   (B) wide
    (C) intelligent   (D) old

13. Weird
    (A) strange   (B) great
    (C) unhealthy   (D) typical

14. Scared
    (A) happy   (B) sad
    (C) angry   (D) afraid

15. Sure
    (A) likely   (B) doubtful
    (C) certain   (D) smart

16. Fair
    (A) just
    (B) large
    (C) loose
    (D) unbalanced
17. Hilarious
    (A) smart
    (B) funny
    (C) small
    (D) large
18. Amazing
    (A) irregular
    (B) crazy
    (C) incredible
    (D) equal
19. Difficult
    (A) soft
    (B) easy
    (C) hard
    (D) old
20. Packed
    (A) alone
    (B) light
    (C) crowded
    (D) heavy

II. Choose the correct synonym to replace the underlined word in the following sentences.

21. After watching the alien movie, Parth started believing that one by one everyone would be <u>abducted</u> by aliens.
    (A) kidnapped
    (B) shortened
    (C) blamed
    (D) obtained
22. Sarah could not believe her mother would actually get her all the things she wanted for her birthday. She kept staring in <u>wonder</u>.
    (A) plentiful
    (B) sudden
    (C) amazement
    (D) enough
23. It is never a good idea to pick up a fight with the persons in <u>authority</u>. You never know what they are capable of.
    (A) large
    (B) power
    (C) reason
    (D) middle
24. I hate it when someone gives away the <u>ending</u> of the book I am still reading.
    (A) story
    (B) cheat
    (C) reveal
    (D) conclusion
25. It's easier to <u>teach</u> children than to teach adults.
    (A) attempt
    (B) educate
    (C) bright
    (D) discover

Fill in the blanks with correct antonym of the word(s) given in the brackets.

26. The country is ______________ in natural resources. (scarce)
    (A) abundant   (B) present
    (C) kind   (D) good

27. Risking his own life to save the puppy was a ______________ act. (cowardly)
    (A) sweet   (B) kind
    (C) nice   (D) brave

28. I am always skeptical about ___________ money to people. I have had a few bad experiences. (borrowing)
    (A) accepting   (B) lending
    (C) encouraging   (D) good

29. He gazed ______________ longingly at the plane that flew miles over his head. (downward)
    (A) sideways   (B) right
    (C) upward   (D) left

30. His lack of technical ___________ kept him from being promoted. (ignorance)
    (A) knowledge   (B) skills
    (C) seniors   (D) followers

—————Darken Your Choice with HB Pencil—————

1.	Ⓐ Ⓑ Ⓒ Ⓓ	7.	Ⓐ Ⓑ Ⓒ Ⓓ	13.	Ⓐ Ⓑ Ⓒ Ⓓ	19	Ⓐ Ⓑ Ⓒ Ⓓ	25.	Ⓐ Ⓑ Ⓒ Ⓓ
2.	Ⓐ Ⓑ Ⓒ Ⓓ	8.	Ⓐ Ⓑ Ⓒ Ⓓ	14.	Ⓐ Ⓑ Ⓒ Ⓓ	20.	Ⓐ Ⓑ Ⓒ Ⓓ	26.	Ⓐ Ⓑ Ⓒ Ⓓ
3.	Ⓐ Ⓑ Ⓒ Ⓓ	9.	Ⓐ Ⓑ Ⓒ Ⓓ	15.	Ⓐ Ⓑ Ⓒ Ⓓ	21.	Ⓐ Ⓑ Ⓒ Ⓓ	27.	Ⓐ Ⓑ Ⓒ Ⓓ
4.	Ⓐ Ⓑ Ⓒ Ⓓ	10.	Ⓐ Ⓑ Ⓒ Ⓓ	16.	Ⓐ Ⓑ Ⓒ Ⓓ	22.	Ⓐ Ⓑ Ⓒ Ⓓ	28.	Ⓐ Ⓑ Ⓒ Ⓓ
5.	Ⓐ Ⓑ Ⓒ Ⓓ	11.	Ⓐ Ⓑ Ⓒ Ⓓ	17.	Ⓐ Ⓑ Ⓒ Ⓓ	23.	Ⓐ Ⓑ Ⓒ Ⓓ	29.	Ⓐ Ⓑ Ⓒ Ⓓ
6.	Ⓐ Ⓑ Ⓒ Ⓓ	12.	Ⓐ Ⓑ Ⓒ Ⓓ	18.	Ⓐ Ⓑ Ⓒ Ⓓ	24.	Ⓐ Ⓑ Ⓒ Ⓓ	30.	Ⓐ Ⓑ Ⓒ Ⓓ

SPELLINGS AND COLLOCATION 2

- ➤ Rules of Spelling
- ➤ Importance of Collocations
- ➤ Types of Collocations

PRACTICE EXERCISE

I. Choose the correct option to replace the incorrect spellings/words given in the following sentences.

1. We reached the hotel quiet late and could not find any accommodation.
   - (A) reachd
   - (B) quite
   - (C) accomodation
   - (D) hotale

2. The chameleon is known for its ability to camoflage itself.
   - (A) chamileon
   - (B) abbility
   - (C) nown
   - (D) camouflage

3. This year our school has decided to focus on the envirement and use of recycled products.
   - (A) school
   - (B) decidead
   - (C) environment
   - (D) recicled

4. The cat knocked down the vace and looked at its owner with mischievous eyes.
   - (A) nocked
   - (B) vase
   - (C) mischevous
   - (D) oner

5. We are having a workshop where we are going to learn correct pronounciation of some difficult words.
   - (A) wokshop
   - (B) corect
   - (C) pronunciation
   - (D) difficult

II. Choose the correctly spelled word/ option for the given expressions.

6. To stop something from burning
   - (A) extinguish
   - (B) estinguish
   - (C) extanguish
   - (D) ecstinguish

7. A feeling of appreciation or thanks
   - (A) grotitude
   - (B) gratatude
   - (C) gratitude
   - (D) gratitute

8. To make very angry or annoy
   - (A) exasparate
   - (B) exasperate
   - (C) ecsasperate
   - (D) exasparade

9. Made up of parts that are different
   - (A) hetrogeneous
   - (B) hatrogeneous
   - (C) heterogenious
   - (D) heterogeneous

10. An area of water that moves in circle
    (A) whirlpull
    (B) whorlpool
    (C) whirlpool
    (D) wirlpool
11. The usual mood of a person
    (A) desposition
    (B) disposition
    (C) disposetion
    (D) dispossession
12. Hard to find
    (A) allusive
    (B) ellusive
    (C) alusive
    (D) elusive
13. The main person or thing
    (A) principle
    (B) principel
    (C) principal
    (D) princepal

III. Choose the correct word/option that completes the given analogy.

14. sun: hot :: ice: ___________
    (A) cold
    (B) cubes
    (C) water
    (D) melt
15. finger: hand :: petal: ___________
    (A) stem
    (B) flower
    (C) garden
    (D) bike
16. eye: see :: ear:
    (A) here
    (B) hearing aid
    (C) hear
    (D) song
17. saw: cut :: hammer:
    (A) screwdiver
    (B) pound
    (C) chainsaw
    (D) screw
18. author: writing :: artist:
    (A) painting
    (B) reading
    (C) typing
    (D) beauty
19. kitchen: house :: keyboard:
    (A) computer
    (B) bedroom
    (C) wires
    (D) classroom
20. city: state :: state:
    (A) country
    (B) continent
    (C) world
    (D) town
21. alive: dead :: awake:
    (A) asleep
    (B) ill
    (C) old
    (D) life
22. smart: clever :: stupid:
    (A) dumb   (B) irritating
    (C) intelligent   (D) quick
23. airplane: flying :: sailboat:
    (A) pilot   (B) sailing
    (C) swimming   (D) fishing
24. child: family :: student:
    (A) class   (B) teacher
    (C) parents   (D) brother
25. bed: sleeping :: pool:
    (A) lifeguard   (B) snoring
    (C) swimming   (D) billiards

I. DIRECTIONS: Find out correct meaning of the following collocations from the given options.

26. Money Laundering

    (A) the crime of processing stolen money through a legitimate business or sending it abroad to a foreign bank, to hide the fact that the money was illegally obtained.

    (B) storing money

    (C) stealing money

    (D) spending money

27. A Round of Applause

    (A) praising somebody

    (B) the noise made by a group of people clapping their hands to show approval

    (C) a token of gratitude

    (D) a note of appreciation

28. Make Coffee

    (A) preparing coffee

    (B) serving coffee

    (C) put on a pot of coffee to serve to drink yourself or serve others

    (D) taking coffee

II. DIRECTIONS: In each of the following questions find out of the alternative which will replace the blank.

29. Film : Audience : : ______:____.

    (A) Novel: Criticism

    (B) Television: Transmission

    (C) Hero : Heroicism

    (D) Radio: Listener

30. Perfection : Flow ::____:____.

    (A) Careless: Mistake

    (B) Anonymity: Identity

    (C) Employee : Colleague

    (D) Book : Notebook

Darken Your Choice with HB Pencil

1.	Ⓐ Ⓑ Ⓒ Ⓓ	7.	Ⓐ Ⓑ Ⓒ Ⓓ	13.	Ⓐ Ⓑ Ⓒ Ⓓ	19	Ⓐ Ⓑ Ⓒ Ⓓ	25.	Ⓐ Ⓑ Ⓒ Ⓓ
2.	Ⓐ Ⓑ Ⓒ Ⓓ	8.	Ⓐ Ⓑ Ⓒ Ⓓ	14.	Ⓐ Ⓑ Ⓒ Ⓓ	20.	Ⓐ Ⓑ Ⓒ Ⓓ	26.	Ⓐ Ⓑ Ⓒ Ⓓ
3.	Ⓐ Ⓑ Ⓒ Ⓓ	9.	Ⓐ Ⓑ Ⓒ Ⓓ	15.	Ⓐ Ⓑ Ⓒ Ⓓ	21.	Ⓐ Ⓑ Ⓒ Ⓓ	27.	Ⓐ Ⓑ Ⓒ Ⓓ
4.	Ⓐ Ⓑ Ⓒ Ⓓ	10.	Ⓐ Ⓑ Ⓒ Ⓓ	16.	Ⓐ Ⓑ Ⓒ Ⓓ	22.	Ⓐ Ⓑ Ⓒ Ⓓ	28.	Ⓐ Ⓑ Ⓒ Ⓓ
5.	Ⓐ Ⓑ Ⓒ Ⓓ	11.	Ⓐ Ⓑ Ⓒ Ⓓ	17.	Ⓐ Ⓑ Ⓒ Ⓓ	23.	Ⓐ Ⓑ Ⓒ Ⓓ	29.	Ⓐ Ⓑ Ⓒ Ⓓ
6.	Ⓐ Ⓑ Ⓒ Ⓓ	12.	Ⓐ Ⓑ Ⓒ Ⓓ	18.	Ⓐ Ⓑ Ⓒ Ⓓ	24.	Ⓐ Ⓑ Ⓒ Ⓓ	30.	Ⓐ Ⓑ Ⓒ Ⓓ

ONE WORD

LEARNING OBJECTIVES

➤ Usage of One Word

PRACTICE EXERCISE

Choose the correct option to describe each of the following expressions.

1. One who looks on the bright side of things
   (A) pessimist   (B) optimistic
   (C) apprentice   (D) atheist

2. One who welcomes guests
   (A) host   (B) guest
   (C) invitee   (D) glutton

3. One who pretends to be what he is not
   (A) cynic   (B) fanatic
   (C) miser   (D) imposter

4. One who observes stars and other objects in space
   (A) connoisseur   (B) astrologer
   (C) astronomer   (D) martyr

5. A four-legged animal
   (A) amphibian   (B) quadruped
   (C) biped   (D) parasite

6. A man who loves mankind and works for the welfare of others
   (A) philanthropist   (B) misanthropist
   (C) plagiarist   (D) feminist

7. One who spends a lot
   (A) miser   (B) mercenary
   (C) spendthrift   (D) cosmopolitan

8. Repeating word for word
   (A) epitaph   (B) verbatim
   (C) oral   (D) linguist

9. A mark that cannot be removed
   (A) incredible   (B) invisible
   (C) invincible   (D) indelible

10. Food that cannot be eaten
    (A) infallible   (B) indelible
    (C) inedible   (D) insatiable

11. A man walking on foot
    (A) pedestrian   (B) veteran
    (C) refugee   (D) amateur

12. A notice of somebody's death
    (A) soliloquy   (B) epitaph
    (C) obituary   (D) post-mortem

13. Someone who cannot read or write
    (A) stoic   (B) bibliophile
    (C) amateur   (D) illiterate

14. Government by the people
    (A) oligarchy   (B) aristocracy
    (C) monocracy   (D) democracy

15. A speech delivered without preparation
    (A) extempore   (B) verbatim
    (C) soliloquy   (D) debate

16. A medicine or drug used to prevent infection
   (A) tablet
   (B) injection
   (C) antiseptic
   (D) vaccine

17. One who expresses himself freely
   (A) introvert
   (B) extrovert
   (C) stoic
   (D) eccentric

18. One who does not believe in god
   (A) novice
   (B) egotist
   (C) monotheist
   (D) atheist

19. One who eats human flesh
   (A) carnivore
   (B) herbivore
   (C) omnivore
   (D) cannibal

20. A work published after the author's death
   (A) plagiarist
   (B) posthumous
   (C) anonymous
   (D) epitaph

HOTS (ACHIEVERS SECTION)

Fill in the blanks with the most suitable word (one word) to complete the following sentences.

21. For a while, my uncle gambled every day, he could not stop himself. He became an _____________.
   (A) addict
   (B) connoisseur
   (C) adamant
   (D) edict

22. My sister works with a reputed newspaper in London. She is a _____________ by profession.
   (A) painter
   (B) author
   (C) journalist
   (D) singer

23. Annie has a huge collection of vinyl records, but the sad part is you cannot play them. The players are _____________ now.
   (A) rare
   (B) expensive
   (C) absolute
   (D) obsolete

24. The bride was shocked to find out on her wedding day that the groom had _______ with his long-time lover.
   (A) eloped
   (B) galloped
   (C) emailed
   (D) eluded

25. The travel agent was yet to share the detailed _____________ with the tourists the day before the departure.
   (A) items
   (B) itinerary
   (C) tertiary
   (D) seminary

_____Darken Your Choice with HB Pencil_____

1.	(A) (B) (C) (D)	6.	(A) (B) (C) (D)	11.	(A) (B) (C) (D)	16	(A) (B) (C) (D)	21.	(A) (B) (C) (D)
2.	(A) (B) (C) (D)	7.	(A) (B) (C) (D)	12.	(A) (B) (C) (D)	17.	(A) (B) (C) (D)	22.	(A) (B) (C) (D)
3.	(A) (B) (C) (D)	8.	(A) (B) (C) (D)	13.	(A) (B) (C) (D)	18.	(A) (B) (C) (D)	23.	(A) (B) (C) (D)
4.	(A) (B) (C) (D)	9.	(A) (B) (C) (D)	14.	(A) (B) (C) (D)	19.	(A) (B) (C) (D)	24.	(A) (B) (C) (D)
5.	(A) (B) (C) (D)	10.	(A) (B) (C) (D)	15.	(A) (B) (C) (D)	20.	(A) (B) (C) (D)	25.	(A) (B) (C) (D)

LEARNING OBJECTIVES

➤ Some common Phrasal verbs
➤ Commonly used Idioms

➤ Uses of Modals
➤ Kinds of Word Order

PRACTICE EXERCISE

I. Fill in the blanks with the correct phrasal verb.

1. It's time to get rid of the old team and _______ in some fresh ideas.
   - (A) set
   - (B) be
   - (C) come
   - (D) bring

2. I'm very unhappy with the service and I intend to _______ in a complaint.
   - (A) cave
   - (B) take
   - (C) dig
   - (D) put

3. When we go to an art museum, it is usually to _________ the works of art.
   - (A) look for
   - (B) look up
   - (C) look after
   - (D) look at

4. I thought my English dictionary was lost, and I _______ it all over the house.
   - (A) looked for
   - (B) looked at
   - (C) looked after
   - (D) look for

5. At the political demonstration the acti-vists were busy _______ tracts against the government.
   - (A) giving out
   - (B) giving up
   - (C) gave out
   - (D) give out

6. When my younger daughter told me she was bored, I told her that she should _______ some sort of sport.
   - (A) go in for
   - (B) go on
   - (C) go round
   - (D) go out for

7. Whenever I want to stop doing these exer-cises, my teacher suggests that I _______.
   - (A) go on
   - (B) go over
   - (C) go out
   - (D) go around

8. We were waiting for our new house, so we were glad that it _______ so fast.
   - (A) went up
   - (B) go up
   - (C) went into
   - (D) go on

9. My parents are taking me to New York for my next holidays; I am really _______ the trip.
   - (A) look forward to
   - (B) looking forward to
   - (C) look forward
   - (D) looked forward to

10. We need to _________ the price of the product, which is relatively high, and focus on its quality as a selling point.
    - (A) back down
    - (B) break down
    - (C) play down
    - (D) settle down

11. Have you ______________ any other interesting product features that we could emphasize in the ads?
   (A) come across   (B) drawn out
   (C) gotten across   (D) made out
12. This poster is horrible and can't be used. The colors and images are all wrong. We will have to __________ .
   (A) do it over   (B) even it out
   (C) do it in   (D) put it down
13. We're going to have to __________ the advertising campaign if we can't get any TV or radio time.
   (A) call on   (B) call off
   (C) drop off   (D) drop out
14. I like that magazine, but I think we should ______________ advertising in it until its circulation has increased.
   (A) put out   (B) put back
   (C) put away   (D) put off
15. My new assistant needs to be __________ before I trust her to run an ad campaign.
   (A) broken down   (B) broken in
   (C) broken up   (D) broken into
16. He started to __________ when he reached the motorway.
   (A) speed off   (B) speed up
   (C) speed away   (D) none of these
17. You need to __________ a form to join the library.
   (A) fill on   (B) fill at
   (C) fill in   (D) none of these
18. The teacher told him to be quiet but he __________ talking.
   (A) Kept up   (B) Kept at
   (C) Kept on   (D) None of these
19. The alarm ___ at 6, but I didn't hear it.
   (A) went out   (B) went away
   (C) went off   (D) none of these
20. The fire was so big that the fire fighters had difficulties in __________ it __________ .

   (A) putting, off   (B) putting, away
   (C) putting, out   (D) none of these

II. Choose the correct meaning of proverb/ idiom. If there is no correct meaning given, (e) 'None of these' will be the answer.

21. To make clean breast of
   (A) To gain prominence
   (B) To praise oneself
   (C) To confess without of reserve
   (D) To destroy before it blooms
   (E) None of these
22. To keeps one's temper
   (A) To become hungry
   (B) To be in good mood
   (C) To preserve one's energy
   (D) To be aloof from
   (E) None of these
23. To catch a tartar
   (A) To trap wanted criminal with great difficulty
   (B) To catch a dangerous person
   (C) To meet with disaster
   (D) To deal with a person who is more than one's match
   (E) None of these
24. To drive home
   (A) To find one's roots
   (B) To return to place of rest
   (C) Back to original position
   (D) To emphasise
   (E) None of these
25. To have an axe to grind
   (A) A private end to serve
   (B) To fail to arouse interest
   (C) To have no result
   (D) To work for both sides
   (E) None of these

I. Fill in the blanks with the correct phrasal verb.

26. If you wish to __________ with Pratap, you need to walk faster.
    (A) catch up   (B) get up
    (C) cheer up   (D) blow up

27. Several years after their fight, the two brothers finally ____________.
    (A) made up   (B) break up
    (C) dress up   (D) hang up

28. I am not being able to __________ his intentions.
    (A) figure up   (B) figure out
    (C) figure in   (D) figure of

29. Sam and Clara's wedding has been ____ for a few days.
    (A) called off   (B) given off
    (C) put off   (D) set off

II. Fill in the blanks with the correct modal.

30. Varsha asked me when I __________ return her book.
    (A) should   (B) will
    (C) must   (D) can

---

1. Ⓐ Ⓑ Ⓒ Ⓓ	7. Ⓐ Ⓑ Ⓒ Ⓓ	13. Ⓐ Ⓑ Ⓒ Ⓓ	19 Ⓐ Ⓑ Ⓒ Ⓓ	25. Ⓐ Ⓑ Ⓒ Ⓓ
2. Ⓐ Ⓑ Ⓒ Ⓓ	8. Ⓐ Ⓑ Ⓒ Ⓓ	14. Ⓐ Ⓑ Ⓒ Ⓓ	20. Ⓐ Ⓑ Ⓒ Ⓓ	26. Ⓐ Ⓑ Ⓒ Ⓓ
3. Ⓐ Ⓑ Ⓒ Ⓓ	9. Ⓐ Ⓑ Ⓒ Ⓓ	15. Ⓐ Ⓑ Ⓒ Ⓓ	21. Ⓐ Ⓑ Ⓒ Ⓓ	27. Ⓐ Ⓑ Ⓒ Ⓓ
4. Ⓐ Ⓑ Ⓒ Ⓓ	10. Ⓐ Ⓑ Ⓒ Ⓓ	16. Ⓐ Ⓑ Ⓒ Ⓓ	22. Ⓐ Ⓑ Ⓒ Ⓓ	28. Ⓐ Ⓑ Ⓒ Ⓓ
5. Ⓐ Ⓑ Ⓒ Ⓓ	11. Ⓐ Ⓑ Ⓒ Ⓓ	17. Ⓐ Ⓑ Ⓒ Ⓓ	23. Ⓐ Ⓑ Ⓒ Ⓓ	29. Ⓐ Ⓑ Ⓒ Ⓓ
6. Ⓐ Ⓑ Ⓒ Ⓓ	12. Ⓐ Ⓑ Ⓒ Ⓓ	18. Ⓐ Ⓑ Ⓒ Ⓓ	24. Ⓐ Ⓑ Ⓒ Ⓓ	30. Ⓐ Ⓑ Ⓒ Ⓓ

NOUNS AND PRONOUNS

LEARNING OBJECTIVES

➤ Nouns and its types
➤ Pronouns and their types

PRACTICE EXERCISE

I. Identify the type of underlined noun and choose the correct option.

1. Always speak the <u>truth</u>.
   (A) Proper   (B) Common
   (C) Collective   (D) Abstract

2. <u>Solomon</u> was the wisest of all kings.
   (A) Proper   (B) Common
   (C) Collective   (D) Abstract

3. <u>Cleanliness</u> is next to godliness.
   (A) Proper   (B) Common
   (C) Collective   (D) Abstract

4. The Nile is the longest of all <u>rivers.</u>
   (A) Proper   (B) Common
   (C) Collective   (D) Abstract

5. Jawaharlal Nehru was the first Prime Minister of <u>India.</u>
   (A) Proper   (B) Common
   (C) Collective   (D) Abstract

6. Birds of a feather <u>flock</u> together.
   (A) Proper   (B) Common
   (C) Collective   (D) Abstract

7. <u>Silver</u> and gold are precious metals.
   (A) Proper   (B) Common
   (C) Collective   (D) Abstract

8. <u>Man</u> pollutes his environment.
   (A) Proper
   (B) Common
   (C) Collective
   (D) Abstract

9. We were delayed because of the <u>traffic</u> jam.
   (A) Proper
   (B) Common
   (C) Collective
   (D) Abstract

10. It was <u>Edison</u> who invented the phonograph.
    (A) Proper   (B) Common
    (C) Collective   (D) Abstract

II. Choose the correct option to fill in the blanks with collective noun.

11. The competition will be judged by a ________________ of experts.
    (A) panel   (B) gang
    (C) army   (D) crew

12. We can see a ________________ of fish swimming in the crystal clear water.
    (A) pride   (B) team
    (C) litter   (D) shoal

13. Whenever there is a street fight, you will see a _________________ of spectators gather around.
(A) pack
(B) pair
(C) crowd
(D) tribe

14. The _______________ of dancers took the stage by storm with their performance.
(A) troupe
(B) group
(C) swarm
(D) troop

15. We saw a _________ of lions in the safari park.
(A) chest
(B) pride
(C) range
(D) flock

16. The children were tired after climbing up a _________ of stairs.
(A) galaxy
(B) fleet
(C) flight
(D) library

17. Marina dropped the ____________ of rice before it reached the table.
(A) stack
(B) piece
(C) basket
(D) bowl

18. The children were happy to look after the ____________ of puppies found in the park.
(A) litter
(B) hive
(C) flock
(D) catch

19. The thieves hid the loot in a ________ of hay.

(A) bunch
(B) stack
(C) bowl
(D) group

20. A ___________ of ships sailed towards the harbor.
(A) string
(B) flight
(C) fleet
(D) herd

III. Choose the correct abstract noun for the given words. The first one is done for you.

21. Agent: ___________
(A) agency (correct answer)
(B) agenda
(C) agents
(D) agentment

22. Act: ___________
(A) acting
(B) actor
(C) actress
(D) action

23. Child: ___________
(A) parent
(B) childhood
(C) playfulness
D) kids

24. Friend: ___________
(A) friends
(B) group
(C) friendship
(D) school

25. Able: ___________
(A) disable
(B) ability
(C) unable
(D) enable

Choose the correct option to fill in the blanks with suitable noun. See the direction given in the brackets.

26. You broke my favourite ____________. (common noun)

    (A) mug   (B) snoopy mug

    (C) natraj   (D) none of these

27. I really want to buy a new pair of ____________. (proper noun)

    (A) jeans   (B) Levis

    (C) clothes   (D) none of these

28. They are all waiting for us at the ________. (common noun)

    (A) McDonalds   (B) restaurant

    (C) dinner set   (D) none of these

29. We are going for tomorrow's cricket match at the ____________. (proper noun)

    (A) Eden Gardens   (B) stadium

    (C) match   (D) none of these

30. There are many patients waiting to see ____________ at the clinic. (common noun)

    (A) Dr. verma   (B) the doctor

    (C) patient   (D) none of these

Darken Your Choice with HB Pencil

1. Ⓐ Ⓑ Ⓒ Ⓓ	7. Ⓐ Ⓑ Ⓒ Ⓓ	13. Ⓐ Ⓑ Ⓒ Ⓓ	19 Ⓐ Ⓑ Ⓒ Ⓓ	25. Ⓐ Ⓑ Ⓒ Ⓓ
2. Ⓐ Ⓑ Ⓒ Ⓓ	8. Ⓐ Ⓑ Ⓒ Ⓓ	14. Ⓐ Ⓑ Ⓒ Ⓓ	20. Ⓐ Ⓑ Ⓒ Ⓓ	26. Ⓐ Ⓑ Ⓒ Ⓓ
3. Ⓐ Ⓑ Ⓒ Ⓓ	9. Ⓐ Ⓑ Ⓒ Ⓓ	15. Ⓐ Ⓑ Ⓒ Ⓓ	21. Ⓐ Ⓑ Ⓒ Ⓓ	27. Ⓐ Ⓑ Ⓒ Ⓓ
4. Ⓐ Ⓑ Ⓒ Ⓓ	10. Ⓐ Ⓑ Ⓒ Ⓓ	16. Ⓐ Ⓑ Ⓒ Ⓓ	22. Ⓐ Ⓑ Ⓒ Ⓓ	28. Ⓐ Ⓑ Ⓒ Ⓓ
5. Ⓐ Ⓑ Ⓒ Ⓓ	11. Ⓐ Ⓑ Ⓒ Ⓓ	17. Ⓐ Ⓑ Ⓒ Ⓓ	23. Ⓐ Ⓑ Ⓒ Ⓓ	29. Ⓐ Ⓑ Ⓒ Ⓓ
6. Ⓐ Ⓑ Ⓒ Ⓓ	12. Ⓐ Ⓑ Ⓒ Ⓓ	18. Ⓐ Ⓑ Ⓒ Ⓓ	24. Ⓐ Ⓑ Ⓒ Ⓓ	30. Ⓐ Ⓑ Ⓒ Ⓓ

VERBS AND ADVERBS

LEARNING OBJECTIVES

➤ Verbs and its types
➤ Basics of Adverbs

➤ Types of Adverbs

PRACTICE EXERCISE

I. **Fill in the blanks with correct form of action verb/option.**

1. My sister ______________ her homework late.
   (A) submitted   (B) submit
   (C) submits   (D) submitting

2. My younger brother ___________ earlier in the night before his test.
   (A) sleep   (B) slept
   (C) sleeping   (D) sleeps

3. The teacher ____________ us in all the remaining problems.
   (A) guide   (B) guides
   (C) guided   (D) guiding

4. The Moon ______________ brightly at night.
   (A) shining   (B) shiny
   (C) shine   (D) shines

5. Manners ______________ a man.
   (A) makes   (B) make
   (C) made   (D) making

6. My sister got me a ______________ doll.
   (A) danced   (B) dances
   (C) dance   (D) dancing

7. ________________ football is not just his hobby, but his profession.
   (A) Played
   (B) Play
   (C) Playing
   (D) Player

8. We ________________ home from the picnic with the setting sun behind us.
   (A) returned
   (B) returning
   (C) return
   (D) returns

9. In order to ______________ early in the morning, you must go to bed early.
   (A) wakes   (B) wake
   (C) waking   (D) awaken

10. We are encouraged ______________ our teeth after every meal.
    (A) to brush   (B) brush
    (C) brushing   (D) brushed

11. I had a hard time staying______________ during the boring speech.
    (A) awoke
    (B) awake
    (C) awaken
    (D) awakened

12. I _________________ to the park today.
    (A) to walk
    (B) walking
    (C) walk
    (D) walked

13. Peter _______________ in China in 1965.
    (A) lived
    (B) lives
    (C) living
    (D) life

14. She goes ___________ every morning.
    (A) run
    (B) running
    (C) ran
    (D) runs

15. My father _______________ a newspaper every day.
    (A) buy
    (B) bought
    (C) buys
    (D) buying

II. Fill in the blanks with suitable verb of being.

16. They ______ visiting their grandmother next month.
    (A) are
    (B) is
    (C) am
    (D) was

17. I __________ looking for a way out of the maze.
    (A) are
    (B) is
    (C) am
    (D) was

18. Last evening, I _____________ looking for my lost dog in the park.
    (A) are
    (B) is
    (C) am
    (D) was

19. The last time we met, you _____________ shopping in the mall.
    (A) were
    (B) is
    (C) am
    (D) was

20. We ___________ painting a house this weekend.
    (A) are
    (B) is
    (C) am
    (D) was

21. My brothers, Niki and Riki, ___________ playing soccer this weekend.
    (A) are
    (B) is
    (C) am
    (D) was

22. Who _________ going to get the grocery this week?
    (A) are
    (B) is
    (C) am
    (D) were

23. It's hard to predict who will win but they _________ putting in their best effort.
    (A) are
    (B) is
    (C) am
    (D) was

24. I did not eat breakfast this morning, so I _________ getting a little hungry now.
    (A) are
    (B) is
    (C) am
    (D) was

25. Compared to my older brother, I ______ much shorter.
    (A) are
    (B) is
    (C) am
    (D) was

I. Fill in the blanks with the correct form of the verb.

26. Had I _______________ his intentions, I _______________ him.
    - (A) know/would avoid
    - (B) knew/avoid
    - (C) known/would have avoided
    - (D) none of these

27. He speaks as though he ______ a lawyer.
    - (A) was
    - (B) is
    - (C) been
    - (D) have

28. Whenever I go to that town, I __________ (make) it a point to visit the church there.
    - (A) make
    - (B) made
    - (C) have made
    - (D) had made

II. Fill in the blanks with the correct adverb.

29. He behaved so _______________ that we were all shocked.
    - (A) strange
    - (B) strangely
    - (C) strangeness
    - (D) stranger

30. Mayank visits his grandparents ______.
    - (A) frequentness
    - (B) frequent
    - (C) frequency
    - (D) frequently

Darken Your Choice with HB Pencil

1.	Ⓐ Ⓑ Ⓒ Ⓓ	7.	Ⓐ Ⓑ Ⓒ Ⓓ	13.	Ⓐ Ⓑ Ⓒ Ⓓ	19	Ⓐ Ⓑ Ⓒ Ⓓ	25.	Ⓐ Ⓑ Ⓒ Ⓓ
2.	Ⓐ Ⓑ Ⓒ Ⓓ	8.	Ⓐ Ⓑ Ⓒ Ⓓ	14.	Ⓐ Ⓑ Ⓒ Ⓓ	20.	Ⓐ Ⓑ Ⓒ Ⓓ	26.	Ⓐ Ⓑ Ⓒ Ⓓ
3.	Ⓐ Ⓑ Ⓒ Ⓓ	9.	Ⓐ Ⓑ Ⓒ Ⓓ	15.	Ⓐ Ⓑ Ⓒ Ⓓ	21.	Ⓐ Ⓑ Ⓒ Ⓓ	27.	Ⓐ Ⓑ Ⓒ Ⓓ
4.	Ⓐ Ⓑ Ⓒ Ⓓ	10.	Ⓐ Ⓑ Ⓒ Ⓓ	16.	Ⓐ Ⓑ Ⓒ Ⓓ	22.	Ⓐ Ⓑ Ⓒ Ⓓ	28.	Ⓐ Ⓑ Ⓒ Ⓓ
5.	Ⓐ Ⓑ Ⓒ Ⓓ	11.	Ⓐ Ⓑ Ⓒ Ⓓ	17.	Ⓐ Ⓑ Ⓒ Ⓓ	23.	Ⓐ Ⓑ Ⓒ Ⓓ	29.	Ⓐ Ⓑ Ⓒ Ⓓ
6.	Ⓐ Ⓑ Ⓒ Ⓓ	12.	Ⓐ Ⓑ Ⓒ Ⓓ	18.	Ⓐ Ⓑ Ⓒ Ⓓ	24.	Ⓐ Ⓑ Ⓒ Ⓓ	30.	Ⓐ Ⓑ Ⓒ Ⓓ

ADJECTIVES

LEARNING OBJECTIVES

➤ Kinds of adjectives
➤ Degree of Comparison

PRACTICE EXERCISE

I. Fill in the blanks with suitable adjective.

1. Make sure you wear a scarf because the weather outside is quite ____________.
    (A) windy   (B) humid
    (C) hot   (D) rainy

2. My new bed not only looks good but is also very ____________.
    (A) heavy   (B) ugly
    (C) comfortable   (D) stiff

3. The little ____________ kitten climbed up the curtains and spilled her milk.
    (A) naughty   (B) lazy
    (C) old   (D) fat

4. We sat and watched as the setting sun created a ____________ sky
    (A) dull
    (B) clear
    (C) gorgeous
    (D) dark

5. I will be performing in front of a large audience tomorrow, so I am feeling ____________.
    (A) angry
    (B) anxious
    (C) jealous
    (D) sleepy

6. The younger sister felt ____________ as the elder one was being showered with presents on her birthday.
    (A) foolish   (B) wise
    (C) jealous   (D) poor

7. Helping my mother with the chores seemed fun at first, but soon it became ____________.
    (A) relaxed
    (B) tedious
    (C) exciting
    (D) happening

8. She is too ____________ to learn the error of her ways.
    (A) arrogant
    (B) hardworking
    (C) disciplined
    (D) wise

9. She was ____________ to receive the bad news.
    (A) happy   (B) excited
    (C) shocked   (D) elated

10. It was so ____________ of you to offer them help.
    (A) rude   (B) horrible
    (C) kind   (D) terrible

II. Fill in the blanks with the correct form of adjective.

11. Of his three sisters, Susan is the _______.
    (A) old
    (B) elder
    (C) eldest
    (D) None of these

12. Very few books are read_____________ Harry Potter by children.
    (A) as much as
    (B) more than
    (C) most
    (D) None of these

13. Black is the _____________ colour.
    (A) dark
    (B) darker
    (C) darkest
    (D) None of these

14. Maya is the _____________ girl in the class.
    (A) pretty
    (B) prettier
    (C) prettiest
    (D) None of these

15. Tina is _____________ than Priti.
    (A) intelligent
    (B) more intelligent
    (C) most intelligent
    (D) None of these

16. The weather today is _____________ than the weather yesterday, but not as _____________ as it was four days ago.
    (A) worse/bad
    (B) bad/bad
    (C) worse/worse
    (D) None of these

17. The road was _____________than we expected.
    (A) long   (B) longer
    (C) longest   (D) None of these

18. Planes are the _____________ means of travelling today.
    (A) convenient
    (B) more convenient
    (C) most convenient
    (D) None of these

19. These jeans are the _______, in fact they are _____________ than the trousers.
    (A) dirty/dirtier
    (B) dirtiest/dirtier
    (C) dirty/dirty
    (D) None of these

21. A candle gives _____________ light than a lamp.
    (A) little
    (B) less
    (C) least
    (D) None of these

22. That boy is the _____________ runner of all.
    (A) fast
    (B) faster
    (C) fastest
    (D) None of these

22. His badminton skills are me _________, among the players in the team.
    (A) good
    (B) better
    (C) best
    (D) None of these

23. The cake is just as _________as the ice-cream.
    (A) sweet
    (B) sweeter
    (C) sweetest
    (D) None of these

24. Shakespeare is _________ than any other English poet.
    (A) great
    (B) greater
    (C) greatest
    (D) None of these

25. Shakespeare is the _________ of all English poets.
    (A) great
    (B) greater
    (C) greatest
    (D) None of these

Read the following passage and select options that can correctly replace the underlined portions.

26. Malaysia is **Q1** country and is blessed with plenty of rain and sunshine. Many types of trees and plants grow here. These trees bear **Q2**fruits. The 'King of Fruits' is without doubt the durian. It is **Q3** fruit. It has **Q4** skin. Inside, however, the fruit is **Q5**. It has a strong smell. The locals love the durian, but foreigners find the smell hard to bear.

    (A) a tropical, developing, small
    (B) a developing, tropical, small
    (C) A small, tropical, developing
    (D) A small, developing, tropical

27. Malaysia is **Q1** country and is blessed with plenty of rain and sunshine. Many types of trees and plants grow here. These trees bear **Q2** fruits. The 'King of Fruits' is without doubt the durian. It is **Q3** fruit. It has **Q4** skin. Inside, however, the fruit is **Q5**. It has a strong smell. The locals love the durian, but foreigners find the smell hard to bear.

    (a) delicious, sweet, many
    (b) Delicious, many, sweet
    (c) Many, delicious, sweet
    (d) Sweet, delicious, many

28. Malaysia is **Q1** country and is blessed with plenty of rain and sunshine. Many types of trees and plants grow here.

These trees bear **Q2** fruits. The 'King of Fruits' is without doubt the durian. It is **Q3** fruit. It has **Q4** skin. Inside, however, the fruit is **Q5**. It has a strong smell. The locals love the durian, but foreigners find the smell hard to bear.

    (a) big, oval-shaped, a
    (b) An oval-shaped, big
    (c) A big, oval-shaped
    (d) The oval-shaped, big

29. Malaysia is **Q1** country and is blessed with plenty of rain and sunshine. Many types of trees and plants grow here. These trees bear **Q2** fruits. The 'King of Fruits' is without doubt the durian. It is **Q3** fruit. It has **Q4** skin. Inside, however, the fruit is **Q5**. It has a strong smell. The locals love the durian, but foreigners find the smell hard to bear.

    (a) a thorny, green or yellow
    (b) A green or yellow, thorny
    (c) Thorny, a green or yellow
    (d) Green or yellow, a thorny

30. Malaysia is **Q1** country and is blessed with plenty of rain and sunshine. Many types of trees and plants grow here. These trees bear **Q2** fruits. The 'King of Fruits' is without doubt the durian. It is **Q3** fruit. It has **Q4** skin. Inside, however, the fruit is **Q5**. It has a strong smell. The locals love the durian, but foreigners find the smell hard to bear.

    (a) soft, sweet, yellow
    (B) Sweet, soft, yellow
    (C) Sweet, yellow, soft
    (D) Yellow, soft and sweet

————Darken Your Choice with HB Pencil————

1.	Ⓐ Ⓑ Ⓒ Ⓓ	7.	Ⓐ Ⓑ Ⓒ Ⓓ	13.	Ⓐ Ⓑ Ⓒ Ⓓ	19	Ⓐ Ⓑ Ⓒ Ⓓ	25.	Ⓐ Ⓑ Ⓒ Ⓓ
2.	Ⓐ Ⓑ Ⓒ Ⓓ	8.	Ⓐ Ⓑ Ⓒ Ⓓ	14.	Ⓐ Ⓑ Ⓒ Ⓓ	20.	Ⓐ Ⓑ Ⓒ Ⓓ	26.	Ⓐ Ⓑ Ⓒ Ⓓ
3.	Ⓐ Ⓑ Ⓒ Ⓓ	9.	Ⓐ Ⓑ Ⓒ Ⓓ	15.	Ⓐ Ⓑ Ⓒ Ⓓ	21.	Ⓐ Ⓑ Ⓒ Ⓓ	27.	Ⓐ Ⓑ Ⓒ Ⓓ
4.	Ⓐ Ⓑ Ⓒ Ⓓ	10.	Ⓐ Ⓑ Ⓒ Ⓓ	16.	Ⓐ Ⓑ Ⓒ Ⓓ	22.	Ⓐ Ⓑ Ⓒ Ⓓ	28.	Ⓐ Ⓑ Ⓒ Ⓓ
5.	Ⓐ Ⓑ Ⓒ Ⓓ	11.	Ⓐ Ⓑ Ⓒ Ⓓ	17.	Ⓐ Ⓑ Ⓒ Ⓓ	23.	Ⓐ Ⓑ Ⓒ Ⓓ	29.	Ⓐ Ⓑ Ⓒ Ⓓ
6.	Ⓐ Ⓑ Ⓒ Ⓓ	12.	Ⓐ Ⓑ Ⓒ Ⓓ	18.	Ⓐ Ⓑ Ⓒ Ⓓ	24.	Ⓐ Ⓑ Ⓒ Ⓓ	30.	Ⓐ Ⓑ Ⓒ Ⓓ

ARTICLES AND PREPOSITIONS 

LEARNING OBJECTIVES

➤ Different articles and their usage
➤ Concept of Preposition

PRACTICE EXERCISE

Fill in the blanks with the correct article. Write 'None' where no article is required.

1. India is one of _______ largest countries in the world.
   - (A) the
   - (B) a
   - (C) an
   - (D) none

2. I never watch _______ television.
   - (A) the
   - (B) a
   - (C) an
   - (D) none

3. In fact, I haven't got _______ television.
   - (A) the
   - (B) a
   - (C) an
   - (D) none

4. _______ Taj Mahal is _______ popular tourist attraction.
   - (A) The/a
   - (B) A/a
   - (C) The/the
   - (D) None/the

5. _______ New Delhi is _______ capital of India.
   - (A) The/the
   - (B) none/the
   - (C) none/a
   - (D) none

6. They went for _______ walk around _______ park nearby.
   - (A) the/a
   - (B) a/the
   - (C) a/an
   - (D) the/none

7. _______ hotel where they held their wedding reception was called _______ Grand Hotel.
   - (A) The/a
   - (B) The/the
   - (C) A/a
   - (D) None/the

8. Ananya was born in _______ India, but she lives in _______ USA now.
   - (A) the/the
   - (B) none/none
   - (C) an/the
   - (D) none/the

9. My father's favourite newspaper is _______ Times of India.
   - (A) the
   - (B) a
   - (C) an
   - (D) none

10. He went on _______ expensive holiday to _______ Andamans.
    - (A) The/the
    - (B) a/the
    - (C) an/the
    - (D) none/none

11. _______ Gateway of India is in _______ Mumbai.
    - (A) The/the
    - (B) A/the
    - (C) The/none
    - (D) None/the

12. Which is _______ highest mountain in _______ world?
    - (A) the/the
    - (B) a/the
    - (C) an/the
    - (D) none/the

13. We had _______ very nice meal. _______ eggs were specially good.
    - (A) the/The
    - (B) a/An
    - (C) a/The
    - (D) none/An

14. New York is _______ exciting city, full of _______ adventures.
    - (A) a/an
    - (B) an/an
    - (C) an/none
    - (D) none/an

15. The company I work with has __________ offices all over India.
(A) the
(B) a
(C) an
(D) none

16. I have two brothers: one of them is still in ______________ college and the other one has ____________ graduated.
(A) the/none
(B) a/none
(C) a/a
(D) none/none

17. He told me that he met __________ alien once from ____________ outer space.
(A) the/an
(B) an/an
(C) an/the
(D) none/an

18. That's __________ hard story to believe.
(A) the
(B) a
(C) an
(D) none

19. My uncle, __________ elderly man is __________ honest person.
(A) an/a
(B) a/a
(C) an/an
(D) none/none

20. He once saved ____________ one-year-old boy from __________ fire.

(A) a/none
(B) a/the
(C) an/the
(D) none/the

21. Look at ____________ apples on that tree. They are so large.
(A) the
(B) a
(C) an
(D) none

22. ______________ life would be very difficult without ____________ electricity.
(A) none/the
(B) none/a
(C) none/an
(D) none/none

23. Are you interested in __________art or __________ architecture?
(A) a/none
(B) none/a
(C) none/none
(D) an/an

24. __________ violence is never justified.
(A) the
(B) a
(C) an
(D) none

25. I would love to live near ____________ sea.
(A) the
(B) a
(C) an
(D) none

HOTS (ACHIEVERS SECTION)

Fill in the blanks with suitable preposition.

26. We must be kind ____________ strangers.
(A) to
(B) for
(C) from
(D) on

27. ______________ of being fined, he was sent to prison.
(A) to
(B) instead
(C) from
(D) on

28. I apologized Akash __________ my rudeness __________ him.
(A) to, for
(B) for, towards
(C) from, on
(D) on, to

29. In scientific experiments _____ accuracy is essential and John could not judge _____ accuracy of the calculations.
(A) an, the
(B) no article, an
(C) no article, the
(D) no article, no article

30. Water is necessary for _____ life but _____ life of these insects does not depend on water.
(A) no article, no article
(B) no article the
(C) the, the
(D) a, the

─────Darken Your Choice with HB Pencil─────

1. Ⓐ Ⓑ Ⓒ Ⓓ	7. Ⓐ Ⓑ Ⓒ Ⓓ	13. Ⓐ Ⓑ Ⓒ Ⓓ	19. Ⓐ Ⓑ Ⓒ Ⓓ	25. Ⓐ Ⓑ Ⓒ Ⓓ
2. Ⓐ Ⓑ Ⓒ Ⓓ	8. Ⓐ Ⓑ Ⓒ Ⓓ	14. Ⓐ Ⓑ Ⓒ Ⓓ	20. Ⓐ Ⓑ Ⓒ Ⓓ	26. Ⓐ Ⓑ Ⓒ Ⓓ
3. Ⓐ Ⓑ Ⓒ Ⓓ	9. Ⓐ Ⓑ Ⓒ Ⓓ	15. Ⓐ Ⓑ Ⓒ Ⓓ	21. Ⓐ Ⓑ Ⓒ Ⓓ	27. Ⓐ Ⓑ Ⓒ Ⓓ
4. Ⓐ Ⓑ Ⓒ Ⓓ	10. Ⓐ Ⓑ Ⓒ Ⓓ	16. Ⓐ Ⓑ Ⓒ Ⓓ	22. Ⓐ Ⓑ Ⓒ Ⓓ	28. Ⓐ Ⓑ Ⓒ Ⓓ
5. Ⓐ Ⓑ Ⓒ Ⓓ	11. Ⓐ Ⓑ Ⓒ Ⓓ	17. Ⓐ Ⓑ Ⓒ Ⓓ	23. Ⓐ Ⓑ Ⓒ Ⓓ	29. Ⓐ Ⓑ Ⓒ Ⓓ
6. Ⓐ Ⓑ Ⓒ Ⓓ	12. Ⓐ Ⓑ Ⓒ Ⓓ	18. Ⓐ Ⓑ Ⓒ Ⓓ	24. Ⓐ Ⓑ Ⓒ Ⓓ	30. Ⓐ Ⓑ Ⓒ Ⓓ

CONJUNCTIONS AND TENSES

LEARNING OBJECTIVES

➤ Conjunctions and its different types
➤ Different Punctuations
➤ Usage of Tenses and its different types

PRACTICE EXERCISE

I. Fill in the blanks with the correct conjunction.

1. It was raining heavily, _____ we decided to cancel our dinner plans.
    (A) so   (B) for
    (C) or   (D) but

2. She wanted to participate in the school play __________ her father would not let her.
    (A) so   (B) for
    (C) or   (D) but

3. I did not go to the show __________ I had already seen it.
    (A) so   (B) as
    (C) or   (D) but

4. Read over your answers ______ correct all mistakes before you pass them up.
    (A) so   (B) for
    (C) and   (D) but

5. She had an unpleasant experience _____ she was in London.
    (A) when   (B) although
    (C) that   (D) if

6. Joy welcomed his guests __________ offered them drinks.

    (A) so   (B) for
    (C) or   (D) and

7. She could not find the book she wanted __________ she borrowed a magazine instead.
    (A) so   (B) for
    (C) or   (D) but

8. Those village folks are poor __________ they seem contended always.
    (A) until   (B) though
    (C) unless   (D) because

9. __________ she hears she won, she will jump with joy.
    (A) if   (B) for
    (C) or   (D) but

10. I don't think he will remember to wish me __________ you remind him.
    (A) so   (B) if
    (C) until   (D) unless

II. Fill in the blanks with the correct form of present tense.

11. I have __________ with me all the necessary books.
    (A) brought   (B) bring
    (C) will bring (D) bringing

12. We _____________ a party last week.
    (A) hold
    (B) held
    (C) will hold
    (D) will be holding
13. We ___________ our breakfast before we ___________ for school.
    (A) eat/left
    (B) ate/left
    (C) ate/leave
    (D) eaten/left
14. The tree that had ___________ on the roof ___________ much damage.
    (A) fall/cause
    (B) fell/caused
    (C) fallen/caused
    (D) fall/caused
15. They _______________ judo in the hall now.
    (A) are practicing
    (B) were practicing
    (C) practiced
    (D) practice
16. I think he has seen us, and he ________ towards us.
    (A) come
    (B) came
    (C) is coming
    (D) will come
17. While the teacher ___________, a lazy boy _____________ at the back of the class.
    (A) taught/slept
    (B) teach/sleep
    (C) was teaching/was sleeping
    (D) will have taught/will have slept
18. It is a pity that Jenny _________ again.
    (A) fail
    (B) failing
    (C) has failed
    (D) had failed
19. Many people __________ this picture.
    (A) has never see
    (B) never see
    (C) never saw
    (D) have never seen
20. I hear that you just _______________ your birthday?
    (A) celebrate
    (B) will celebrate
    (C) celebrating
    (D) celebrated
21. Did you _____________ many friends?
    (A) invited
    (B) inviting
    (C) invite
    (D) invitation
22. This is the first time such a thing _______ here.
    (A) happens
    (B) happened
    (C) happen
    (D) happening
23. I think I _______________ my pen.
    (A) lose
    (B) have lost
    (C) has lost
    (D) will lost
24. We __________ friends since childhood.
    (A) been
    (B) has been
    (C) have been
    (D) will be
25. This computer _______________ with us for only a month.
    (A) have been
    (B) has been
    (C) will been
    (D) been

Choose the correct tense of the following sentences.

26. He is sleeping. Do not disturb.
    (A) Present Continuous
    (B) Past Continuous
    (C) Present Perfect
    (D) Past Perfect

27. The sun rises in the east.
    (A) Simple Present   (B) Simple Past
    (C) Simple Future   (D) Present Perfect

28. She enjoys reading books.
    (A) Simple Present   (B) Simple Past
    (C) Simple Future   (D) Present Perfect

29. By the time you reach there, the train would have left.
    (A) Past Perfect   (B) Simple Past
    (C) Future Perfect   (D) Present Perfect

30. By the end of this month, we will have completed the syllabus.
    (A) Past Perfect   (B) Simple Past
    (C) Future Perfect   (D) Present Perfect

1.	Ⓐ Ⓑ Ⓒ Ⓓ	7.	Ⓐ Ⓑ Ⓒ Ⓓ	13.	Ⓐ Ⓑ Ⓒ Ⓓ	19	Ⓐ Ⓑ Ⓒ Ⓓ	25.	Ⓐ Ⓑ Ⓒ Ⓓ
2.	Ⓐ Ⓑ Ⓒ Ⓓ	8.	Ⓐ Ⓑ Ⓒ Ⓓ	14.	Ⓐ Ⓑ Ⓒ Ⓓ	20.	Ⓐ Ⓑ Ⓒ Ⓓ	26.	Ⓐ Ⓑ Ⓒ Ⓓ
3.	Ⓐ Ⓑ Ⓒ Ⓓ	9.	Ⓐ Ⓑ Ⓒ Ⓓ	15.	Ⓐ Ⓑ Ⓒ Ⓓ	21.	Ⓐ Ⓑ Ⓒ Ⓓ	27.	Ⓐ Ⓑ Ⓒ Ⓓ
4.	Ⓐ Ⓑ Ⓒ Ⓓ	10.	Ⓐ Ⓑ Ⓒ Ⓓ	16.	Ⓐ Ⓑ Ⓒ Ⓓ	22.	Ⓐ Ⓑ Ⓒ Ⓓ	28.	Ⓐ Ⓑ Ⓒ Ⓓ
5.	Ⓐ Ⓑ Ⓒ Ⓓ	11.	Ⓐ Ⓑ Ⓒ Ⓓ	17.	Ⓐ Ⓑ Ⓒ Ⓓ	23.	Ⓐ Ⓑ Ⓒ Ⓓ	29.	Ⓐ Ⓑ Ⓒ Ⓓ
6.	Ⓐ Ⓑ Ⓒ Ⓓ	12.	Ⓐ Ⓑ Ⓒ Ⓓ	18.	Ⓐ Ⓑ Ⓒ Ⓓ	24.	Ⓐ Ⓑ Ⓒ Ⓓ	30.	Ⓐ Ⓑ Ⓒ Ⓓ

VOICES AND NARRATION

LEARNING OBJECTIVES

➤ Active Voice
➤ Passive Voice
➤ Direct and Indirect Speech

PRACTICE EXERCISE

Choose the option which contains the correct passive/active voice of the given sentence.

1. He can speak French.
   - (A) French can spoken by him.
   - (B) French can be spoke by him.
   - (C) French can be spoken by him.
   - (D) French could be spoken by him.

2. They may win the battle.
   - (A) The battle may be win.
   - (B) The battle may be won.
   - (C) The battle may be won by them.
   - (D) The battle may won.

3. Nobody can catch him.
   - (A) He can not be caught.
   - (B) He can not caught.
   - (C) He could not be cought.
   - (D) He could not cought.

4. We must have obeyed our teachers.
   - (A) Our teachers might have obeyed.
   - (B) Our teachers might have been obeyed.
   - (C) Our teachers must have been obeyed.
   - (D) Our teachers must have obeyed.

5. Rahul must have done that task.
   - (A) That task must had been done by Rahul.
   - (B) That task must have been done by Rahul.
   - (C) That task must have done by Rahul.
   - (D) That task must have been did by Rahul.

6. We ought to have saved our environment.
   - (A) Our environment ought to had been saved.
   - (B) Our environment ought to have been save.
   - (C) Our environment ought to have been saved.
   - (D) Our environment ought to have saved.

7. There is no book to read.
   - (A) To be read there is no book.
   - (B) To read there is no book.
   - (C) There is no book to read.
   - (D) There is no book to be read.

8. There is nothing to do.
   - (A) There was nothing to be done.
   - (B) There is nothing to be done.
   - (C) There is nothing to done.
   - (D) There is no thing to do.

9. It is time to prepare for the game trails.
   - (A) It is time to prepared for the game trails.

(B) It is time to be prepared for the game trails.
(C) It is time for the game trails to prepared.
(D) It is time for the game trails to be prepared.

10. It is time to learn English.
(A) It is time to be learnt English.
(B) It is time for English to be learnt.
(C) It is time for English to learnt.
(D) It is time to be learn English.

11. It is time to do our business.
(A) It is time for our business to be done.
(B) It is time to our business to be done.
(C) It is time our business to be done.
(D) It is time for our business be done.

12. He likes people to respect him.
(A) He like respect.
(B) He likes to be respected.
(C) He like to be respected.
(D) He want to be respected.

13. Rohit has to see it or to believe it.
(A) It has to be saw or to be believe by Rohit.
(B) It has to be seen or to believe by Rohit.
(C) It has to be seen or to be believed by Rohit.
(D) It has to be seen or to be believe by Rohit.

14. Switch on the cooler.
(A) Let cooler be switch on.
(B) Switch on the cooler please.
(C) Let cooler be switched on.
(D) Let the cooler be switched on.

15. Bring the bottle of juice.
(A) Let a bottle of juice be brought.
(B) Let the bottle of juice be brought.
(C) Let a bottle of juice brought.
(D) Let a bottle of juice be bring.

16. Don't insult the deaf man.
(A) Let the deaf man not be insult.
(B) Let the deaf man not be insulted.
(C) Let the deaf man not insulted.
(D) Let deaf man not be insulted.

17. Don't touch the fence.
(A) Let the fence not be touch.
(B) Let the fence not be touched.
(C) Let the fence not touched.
(D) Let the fence to not be touched.

18. Help the poor.
(A) The poor should helped.
(B) We should help poor.
(C) Let the poor be helped.
(D) The poor should be helped.

19. Respect your neighbours.
(A) Your neighbours should respected.
(B) Your neighbours should be respected.
(C) Let neighbours be respected.
(D) Let neighbours respected.

20. Please give me a pen.
(A) You are ordered to give me a pen.
(B) You are ought to give me a pen.
(C) You are requested to give me pen.
(D) You are requested to give me a pen.

21. Please tell me something.
(A) You are requested to tell me something.
(B) You are requested tell me something.
(C) You are requested to tell something.
(D) You are request to tell me something.

22. This shirt cannot be worn by me any longer.
(A) I cannot wear this shirt any longer.
(B) Wearing of this shirt any longer is not possible.
(C) This shirt is too worn out any longer.
(D) This worn out shirt cannot be worn any longer.

23. Lion does not eat grass, however hungry he may be.

(A) Grass is not eaten by a lion, however hungry he may be.
(B) Grass was being not eaten by a lion, however hungry he may be.
(C) Grass is eaten not by a lion, however hungry he may be.
(D) Grass is not being eaten by a lion, however hungry he may be.

24. Someone saw him picking up a gun.
    (A) He was seen pick up a gun by someone.
    (B) He was seen picking up a gun by someone.
    (C) He is seen picking up a gun by someone.
    (D) He was seen by someone pick a gun.

25. He was obliged to resign.
    (A) He was make to resign.
    (B) To resign was his obligation.
    (C) Circumstances obliged him to resign.
    (D) Registration obliged him.

HOTS (ACHIEVERS SECTION)

Direction: Choose the most suitable passive voice conversions of the given sentences:

26. The manager will give you a ticket.
    (A) A ticket will be given to you by the manager.
    (B) You will be given a ticket by the manager.
    (C) Both (a) and (b)
    (D) None of the above.

27. We saw you and him.
    (A) You and him was seen by us.
    (B) You and he were seen by us.
    (C) You and him were seen by us.
    (D) You and he seen by us.

28. Give the order for one hundred calendars.
    (A) Let the order for one hundred calendars be given.
    (B) Order for one hundred calendars should be given.
    (C) Both (a) and (b)
    (D) None of the above.

29. Call the ambulance at once.
    (A) Let the ambulance called at once.
    (B) The ambulance should be called at once.
    (C) Let the ambulance be called at once.
    (D) Both (b) and (c)

30. Mrs. Smith looks after her children very well.
    (A) Her children looked very well by Mrs. Smith.
    (B) Her children are looked very well by Mrs. Smith.
    (C) Her children are looked after very well by Mrs. Smith.
    (D) None of these

—Darken Your Choice with HB Pencil—

1.	Ⓐ Ⓑ Ⓒ Ⓓ	7.	Ⓐ Ⓑ Ⓒ Ⓓ	13.	Ⓐ Ⓑ Ⓒ Ⓓ	19	Ⓐ Ⓑ Ⓒ Ⓓ	25.	Ⓐ Ⓑ Ⓒ Ⓓ
2.	Ⓐ Ⓑ Ⓒ Ⓓ	8.	Ⓐ Ⓑ Ⓒ Ⓓ	14.	Ⓐ Ⓑ Ⓒ Ⓓ	20.	Ⓐ Ⓑ Ⓒ Ⓓ	26.	Ⓐ Ⓑ Ⓒ Ⓓ
3.	Ⓐ Ⓑ Ⓒ Ⓓ	9.	Ⓐ Ⓑ Ⓒ Ⓓ	15.	Ⓐ Ⓑ Ⓒ Ⓓ	21.	Ⓐ Ⓑ Ⓒ Ⓓ	27.	Ⓐ Ⓑ Ⓒ Ⓓ
4.	Ⓐ Ⓑ Ⓒ Ⓓ	10.	Ⓐ Ⓑ Ⓒ Ⓓ	16.	Ⓐ Ⓑ Ⓒ Ⓓ	22.	Ⓐ Ⓑ Ⓒ Ⓓ	28.	Ⓐ Ⓑ Ⓒ Ⓓ
5.	Ⓐ Ⓑ Ⓒ Ⓓ	11.	Ⓐ Ⓑ Ⓒ Ⓓ	17.	Ⓐ Ⓑ Ⓒ Ⓓ	23.	Ⓐ Ⓑ Ⓒ Ⓓ	29.	Ⓐ Ⓑ Ⓒ Ⓓ
6.	Ⓐ Ⓑ Ⓒ Ⓓ	12.	Ⓐ Ⓑ Ⓒ Ⓓ	18.	Ⓐ Ⓑ Ⓒ Ⓓ	24.	Ⓐ Ⓑ Ⓒ Ⓓ	30.	Ⓐ Ⓑ Ⓒ Ⓓ

OLYMPIAD WORKBOOK (IEO) CLASS– 7

VOCABULARY

LEARNING OBJECTIVES

➤ Words related to travel, leisure, locations and Activities

PRACTICE EXERCISE

I. Fill in the blanks with the most appropriate word.

1. _____________ are quite high these days. But they are often slashed during the festive seasons.
   - (A) airfares
   - (B) international
   - (C) hotel
   - (D) passport

2. My uncle is a _____________. He travelled to fifteen countries in the past six months.
   - (A) passenger
   - (B) tourist
   - (C) globetrotter
   - (D) travel agent

3. I have signed up for an _____________ to Mt Everest. However, I need to go through some physical training before that.
   - (A) sightseeing
   - (B) expedition
   - (C) voyage
   - (D) vacation

4. The main attraction of the Jim Corbett National Park is the wildlife _________.
   - (A) tour
   - (B) ferry
   - (C) cruise
   - (D) safari

5. We usually say _________ to a person setting off on a journey.
   - (A) bon voyage
   - (B) check in
   - (C) take off
   - (D) sail

6. I came to the mountains because I love _____________ up the hills on foot.
   - (A) biking
   - (B) hiking
   - (C) skiing
   - (D) riding

7. My parents have visited all the states in India. Next year they are planning to go _____________.
   - (A) board
   - (B) road
   - (C) route
   - (D) abroad

8. She caught the last _____________ across the river just before sunset.
   - (A) taxi
   - (B) train
   - (C) ferry
   - (D) bus

9. In order to cut down expenditure, Jess decided to not stay in a _____________, but go _____________ instead.
   - (A) hotel/camping
   - (B) camp/hotel
   - (C) hotel/resort
   - (D) hotel/boathouse

10. There's a new bird _____________ near my house. You can spot many rare species there.
    - (A) safari
    - (B) sanctuary
    - (C) destination
    - (D) lodging

II. **Fill in the blanks with the correct option.**

11. Standing at the edge of the ___________, we watched the waves crash on the shore far below.
    (A) cliff   (B) beach
    (C) lake   (D) port

12. In the evenings, he loves to watch the children play in the ___________ across the street.
    (A) road   (B) country
    (C) park   (D) forest

13. The authorities have decided to cut down the ___________ to make way for a new roadway.
    (A) hill   (B) forest
    (C) river   (D) sea

14. I visited a ___________ this morning where the priest was a woman.
    (A) city   (B) town
    (C) park   (D) church

15. New Delhi is to India, like London is to United Kingdom. They are the _______ cities.
    (A) capital   (B) country
    (C) city   (D) countryside

16. According to the weather forecast, the typhoon is likely to approach the _______.
    (A) residence   (B) district
    (C) coast   (D) bay

17. Although considered to be a holy _______, not enough is done to keep the Ganges clean.
    (A) river   (B) town
    (C) city   (D) coast

18. Tom baked over a 100 cupcakes this after noon. He plans to open a _______ of his own very soon.
    (A) hospital   (B) bakery
    (C) school   (D) post office

19. I waited at the ___________ for more than an hour to lodge a complaint against the robbery at my apartment.
    (A) school   (B) restaurant
    (C) post office   (D) police station

20. These days, people prefer to go to ______ more than meeting up with friends and relatives.
    (A) cottage   (B) shopping mall
    (C) outskirts   (D) port

III. **Choose the correct option which describes the given expression.**

21. A very tall building in a city
    (A) school   (B) post office
    (C) skyscraper   (D) block

22. A place where sick or injured people are given care or treatment
    (A) house   (B) hospital
    (C) church   (D) resort

23. An area of low land between hills or mountains
    (A) valley   (B) beach
    (C) coast   (D) stream

24. Relating to country, rather than city
    (A) urban   (B) forest
    (C) outskirts   (D) rural

25. A large building with high, thick walls and towers that was built in the past to protect against attack
    (A) church
    (B) cathedral
    (C) castle
    (D) cottage

Choose the correct option (in column B) which describes the given picture (in column A)

S. No	Column A	Column B
26.		(A) roll (B) twist (C) crawl (d) tiptoe
27.		(A) swim (B) dive (C) dig (S) jump
28.		(A) kick (B) run (C) leap (D) hop
29.		(A) sway (B) wave (C) swirl (D) dance

| 30. | | (A) roll
(B) skate
(C) ride
(D) shuffle |

1.	Ⓐ Ⓑ Ⓒ Ⓓ	7.	Ⓐ Ⓑ Ⓒ Ⓓ	13.	Ⓐ Ⓑ Ⓒ Ⓓ	19	Ⓐ Ⓑ Ⓒ Ⓓ	25.	Ⓐ Ⓑ Ⓒ Ⓓ
2.	Ⓐ Ⓑ Ⓒ Ⓓ	8.	Ⓐ Ⓑ Ⓒ Ⓓ	14.	Ⓐ Ⓑ Ⓒ Ⓓ	20.	Ⓐ Ⓑ Ⓒ Ⓓ	26.	Ⓐ Ⓑ Ⓒ Ⓓ
3.	Ⓐ Ⓑ Ⓒ Ⓓ	9.	Ⓐ Ⓑ Ⓒ Ⓓ	15.	Ⓐ Ⓑ Ⓒ Ⓓ	21.	Ⓐ Ⓑ Ⓒ Ⓓ	27.	Ⓐ Ⓑ Ⓒ Ⓓ
4.	Ⓐ Ⓑ Ⓒ Ⓓ	10.	Ⓐ Ⓑ Ⓒ Ⓓ	16.	Ⓐ Ⓑ Ⓒ Ⓓ	22.	Ⓐ Ⓑ Ⓒ Ⓓ	28.	Ⓐ Ⓑ Ⓒ Ⓓ
5.	Ⓐ Ⓑ Ⓒ Ⓓ	11.	Ⓐ Ⓑ Ⓒ Ⓓ	17.	Ⓐ Ⓑ Ⓒ Ⓓ	23.	Ⓐ Ⓑ Ⓒ Ⓓ	29.	Ⓐ Ⓑ Ⓒ Ⓓ
6.	Ⓐ Ⓑ Ⓒ Ⓓ	12.	Ⓐ Ⓑ Ⓒ Ⓓ	18.	Ⓐ Ⓑ Ⓒ Ⓓ	24.	Ⓐ Ⓑ Ⓒ Ⓓ	30.	Ⓐ Ⓑ Ⓒ Ⓓ

SEQUENCING-STORIES, EVENTS AND SNIPPETS

LEARNING OBJECTIVES

➤ Sequencing Stories
➤ Sequencing Events

PRACTICE EXERCISE

1. Read the following sentences and answer the questions that follow:
   i. A hunter, however, comes to the rescue and cuts the wolf open. Immediately, Little Red Riding Hood and her grandmother emerge unharmed.
   ii. This tale is about a girl called Little Red Riding Hood, she always wears the red hooded cape. Every day, the girl walks through the woods to deliver food to her grandmother.
   iii. One day, a wolf approaches the girl and she naively tells him where she is going.
   iv. In the meantime, the wolf goes to the grandmother's house and eats her. When the girl arrives he eats her too.
   v. He suggests the girl to pick some flowers for her grandmother who was keeping unwell. She does so.

   Arrange the above sentences in a logical order to form a meaningful story.
   (A) i-ii-iii-iv-v   (B) ii-iii-v-iv-i
   (C) ii-i-iv-v-iii   (D) ii-iv-i-iii-v

2. Read the following sentences and answer the questions that follow:
   i. A hunter, however, comes to the rescue and cuts the wolf open. Immediately, Little Red Riding Hood and her grandmother emerge unharmed.
   ii. This tale is about a girl called Little Red Riding Hood, she always wears the red hooded cape. Every day, the girl walks through the woods to deliver food to her grandmother.
   iii. One day, a wolf approaches the girl and she naively tells him where she is going.
   iv. In the meantime, the wolf goes to the grandmother's house and eats her. When the girl arrives he eats her too.
   v. He suggests the girl to pick some flowers for her grandmother who was keeping unwell. She does so.

   What is the moral of the story?
   (A) Always meet your grandmother in the forest,
   (B) Never listen to strangers.
   (C) Never be friends with a wolf.
   (D) Never tell the truth.

3. Read each of the following sentences and arrange them in a logical order:
   i. His relatives live in London, but they are coming for the wedding. All of Sakshi's family live right here in

Mumbai. The wedding ceremony is scheduled to take place in Udaipur.

   ii. She is going to marry Sachin Sharma who lives in the USA.

  iii. After marriage, Sakshi would be travelling to the USA, where she already has a job

  iv. Sakshi Mittal is getting married in June.

(A) iv-ii-i-iii   (B) iv-i-ii-iii
(C) ii-i-iv-iii   (D) i-ii-iv-iii

4. Read each of the following sentences and arrange them in a logical order:
   i. Her dance performances are like fairy tales and she moves like a fairy.
   ii. In these fairy tales, she tells us about legends from the stories of ancient India
  iii. My dance teacher is an Indian classical dancer.
  iv. She was born in England but as a dancer, she learnt her technique in the North-vast India from a famous master.

(A) iii-iv-i-ii   (B) i-iv-iii-ii
(C) i-ii-iii-iv   (D) iv-i-ii-iii

5. Read each of the following sentences and arrange them in a logical order:
   i. This man got the job
   ii. Along the corridor, he picked up a piece of paper and threw it in the dustbin.
  iii. A man attended an interview for a job.
  iv. The interviewer passed by and saw it.

(A) iii-ii-iv-i   (B) iii-ii-i-iv
(C) iii-iv-ii-i   (D) iii-i-ii-iv

6. Read each of the following sentences and arrange them in a logical order:
   i. I had two eggs, a piece of toast and a glass of orange juice.
   ii. I woke up one morning to a beautiful sunrise.
  iii. I was very hungry that morning, so I headed for the breakfast table.
  iv. After breakfast, I ran to the bus stop for an other glorious day of school

(A) i-ii-iii-iv   (B) ii-iii-i-iv
(C) iii-iv-ii-i   (D) iii-i-ii-iv

7. Read each of the following sentences and arrange them in a logical order:
   i. People who live in the city do not have to worry about wells or springs.
   ii. The city supplies them with water.
  iii. For them, water may come from a spring, a well or underground water connection.
  iv. But in villages, especially for farmers, obtaining water supply may be quite a problem.

(A) iii-iv-ii-i   (B) i-ii-iv-iii
(C) ii-iii-iv-i   (D) iii-i-ii-iv

8. Read each of the following sentences and arrange them in a logical order:
   i. This process also reduces the amount of waste going into landfills.
   ii. For making this work we put used materials in a landfill, it is developed and made into new items.
  iii. Lastly, as a result it also helps to bring prices down on items that are made from using recycled waste.
  iv. Recycling is the term used to describe an alternative form of getting rid of used materials.

(A) iii-iv-ii-i   (B) iv-i-ii-iii
(C) iv-iii-ii-i   (D) iv-ii-i-iii

9. Read the following snippets and answer the questions that follow:

In a writing career that spanned more than half a century, Agatha Christie wrote 79 novels and short story collections. What is the meaning of the word 'spanned' as used in the above snippet?

(A) Spin over   (B) Triviality
(C) Extended over   (D) Consequence

10. Read the following snippets and answer the questions that follow:

In 1961, earth tremors began to disturb the islanders. Then, a volcanic eruption forced the evacuation of the entire

population. They were housed at a camp near Southampton. What is the meaning of the word 'evacuation' as used in the above snippet?
(A) Voyage (B) Mass departure
(C) Trek (D) Expedition

11. Read the following snippets and answer the questions that follow:
"The Times has had an excellent reputation for over 200 year," said its editor, who has been working for the paper since 1980, "and now we are trying our best to continue that tradition in order to produce a newspaper for the twenty-first century." What is the meaning of the word 'tradition' as used in the above snippet?
(A) Convention (B) Innovation
(C) Modernisation (D) Advancement

12. Read the following snippets and answer the questions that follow:
I don't always agree with the opinion stated on the editorial page, but it's good to know how other people feel about items in the news. What is the meaning of the word 'opinion' as used in the above snippet?
(A) Significance (B) Importance
(C) View, belief (D) Outcome

13. Read the following snippets and answer the questions that follow:
The joy of our daughter looking through the window to see the familiar surroundings covered with a blanket of untouched white snow, was so exciting that we couldn't resist the temptation to take the journey north into the mountains. Which of the following words is not similar in meaning to 'temptation'?
(A) Enticement (B) Limitation
(C) Appeal (D) Inducement

14. Read the following snippets and answer the questions that follow:
Jane, from Manchester, has been taking in foster pets for more than four years. having been among the first to sign up when 'Paws for Kids' started in March 1999.What is the meaning of 'foster' in the phrase 'foster pets'?
(A) Harm (B) Discourage
(C) To nurture (D) Block

15. Read the following snippets and answer the questions that follow:
Most Europeans live in small villages. They grow their own food and barter with others. As well as keeping animals, they grow small crops of wheat, rye and vegetables. Milk, from dairy cows, is a vital part of the diet. This milk is also used to make butter and cheese. Which of the following words can replace the word 'barter' used above, without changing the meaning of the text?
(A) Traverse (B) Keep
(C) Persuade (D) Exchange

16. Find correct sequence of sentence:
P: youngsters in the cities and the villages
Q: The effect
R: of the cinema
S: on the school and college going is very bad
(A) PRQS (B) QRSP
(C) QPSR (D) RQSP

17. Find correct sequence of sentence :
P: I have not come to complain he said
Q: even if it means some humiliation
R: but the boy must learn to be honest
S: and admit he broke it.
(A) PQRS (B) QRPS
(C) QPRS (D) PRQS

18. Find correct sequence of sentence :
P: not indeed in the sense that education has been universal
Q: Our country has been a land of learning
R: and the learned man has been held in higher esteem than the warrior or administrator
S: but in the sense that education has been universal
(A) QRSP (B) RSPQ
(C) QPSR (D) RQSP

19. Find correct sequence of sentence :
P: appear in examinations
Q: many students from all over India
R: by different organisations
S: which are held on all India basis
(A) QPSR   (B) QRSP
(C) QPRS   (D) PRQS

20. Find the correct sequence of sentences :
P: to protect vegetables from cold
Q: in view of the prevailing weather conditions
R: farmers to smoke their fields during the night
S: agricultural experts have advised
(A) PRQS   (B) QSRP
(C) RPSQ   (D) SPQR

HOTS (ACHIEVERS SECTION)

21. Find the right sequence of sentences :
P: if it was time to go yet
Q: and ran downstairs to see
R: Rahul jumped out of bed
S: on Saturday morning
(A) RPQR   (B) SPRQ
(C) RQSP   (D) SRQP

22. Find the right sequence of sentences:
P: in my heart of hearts
Q: to hear his voice
R: I wasn't sure what I really wished
S: through that window once more
(A) PQRS   (B) RPQS
(C) SRQP   (D) RPSQ

23. Find the correct sequence of sentences :
1: Your letter was big relief.
P : How did you exams go?
Q : After your result, you must come here for a week.
R : You hadn't written for over a month.
S : I am sure you will come out with flying colours.
6: But don't forget to bring chocolate for Geetha.
(A) RPSQ   (B) SQRP
(C) PRQS   (D) PQRS

24. Find the correct sequence of sentences :
1 : I took cigarettes from my case.
P : but when the fit of coughing was over, he replaced it between his lips.
Q : I lit one of them and placed it between the lips.
R : then with a feeble hand he removed the cigarette.
S : slowly he took a pull at it and coughed violently.
6 : Then he continues to draw on it.
(A) RPQS   (B) QSRP
(C) PQRS   (D) QRSP

25. Find the correct sequence of sentences :
Religion has been used
P: both as a weapon of isolation
Q: to dull awareness
R: about real problems
S: and as morphia
6: like education, health and employment
(A) QPSR   (B) PQRS
(C) QRPS   (D) PSQR

Darken Your Choice with HB Pencil

1.	Ⓐ Ⓑ Ⓒ Ⓓ	6.	Ⓐ Ⓑ Ⓒ Ⓓ	11.	Ⓐ Ⓑ Ⓒ Ⓓ	16	Ⓐ Ⓑ Ⓒ Ⓓ	21.	Ⓐ Ⓑ Ⓒ Ⓓ
2.	Ⓐ Ⓑ Ⓒ Ⓓ	7.	Ⓐ Ⓑ Ⓒ Ⓓ	12.	Ⓐ Ⓑ Ⓒ Ⓓ	17.	Ⓐ Ⓑ Ⓒ Ⓓ	22.	Ⓐ Ⓑ Ⓒ Ⓓ
3.	Ⓐ Ⓑ Ⓒ Ⓓ	8.	Ⓐ Ⓑ Ⓒ Ⓓ	13.	Ⓐ Ⓑ Ⓒ Ⓓ	18.	Ⓐ Ⓑ Ⓒ Ⓓ	23.	Ⓐ Ⓑ Ⓒ Ⓓ
4.	Ⓐ Ⓑ Ⓒ Ⓓ	9.	Ⓐ Ⓑ Ⓒ Ⓓ	14.	Ⓐ Ⓑ Ⓒ Ⓓ	19.	Ⓐ Ⓑ Ⓒ Ⓓ	24.	Ⓐ Ⓑ Ⓒ Ⓓ
5.	Ⓐ Ⓑ Ⓒ Ⓓ	10.	Ⓐ Ⓑ Ⓒ Ⓓ	15.	Ⓐ Ⓑ Ⓒ Ⓓ	20.	Ⓐ Ⓑ Ⓒ Ⓓ	25.	Ⓐ Ⓑ Ⓒ Ⓓ

COMPREHENSION

LEARNING OBJECTIVES

➤ Reading Comprehension

PRACTICE EXERCISE

1. What is the magnitude of the terror felt?
    (A) 9.8   (B) 8.9
    (C) 7.8   (D) 8.7

2. A state emergency has been declared at the ______________ nuclear plant.
    (A) Fukushima   (B) Fakashima
    (C) Kukushima   (D) Fikusina

3. The passage talks about another quake that happened a month ago. Where did it take place?
    (A) Australia   (B) China
    (C) Japan   (D) New Zealand

4. How were the crowds behaving after facing the massive quake?
    (A) they were panicking
    (B) there was a stampeded
    (C) they were calm and orderly
    (D) there were fights

5. Where were people spending their nights in Tokyo?
    (A) offices   (B) trains
    (C) homes   (D) rescue centres

6. When was the last time India won the World Cup?
    (A) 1986   (B) 2000
    (C) 1983   (D) 1999

7. How many runs did Mahendra Singh Dhoni score?
    (A) 91   (B) 97
    (C) 100   (D) 95

8. Who scored the winning run?
    (A) Gautam Gambhir
    (B) Mahendra Singh Dhoni
    (C) Sachin Tendulkar
    (D) Gary Kirsten

9. As used in the passage, what does the word 'silverware' mean?
    (A) silver coins
    (B) a new car model
    (C) cutlery
    (D) trophy

10. Who had his farewell on the same day?
    (A) Sachin Tendulkar
    (B) Mahendra Singh Dhoni
    (C) Sourav Ganguly
    (D) Gary Kirsten

11. What has affected the onion production?
    (A) scanty rainfall
    (B) theft from godowns
    (C) pesticides
    (D) farmer suicides

12. Onions have been imported from which two countries?
(A) Egypt and Sudan
(B) Bangladesh and Pakistan
(C) Afghanistan and Pakistan
(D) Pakistan and Egypt

13. How much onion does Mumbai need on a daily basis?
(A) 80–100 trucks each containing 12 tonnes
(B) 12 tonnes
(C) 700 kg
(D) 2,000 kg

14. What is the price of onion at Lasalgaon?
(A) Rs 80 kg
(B) Rs 60 kg
(C) Rs 100 kg
(D) Rs 90 kg

15. As used in the passage, what does the word 'unabated' mean?
(A) without becoming less
(B) decreasing order
(C) diminishing monsoon
(D) shortage

16. Who is looking for reporters?
(A) a TV channel
(B) a newspaper
(C) a radio channel
(D) a magazine

17. Which of these words is a synonym of the word 'reporter'?
(A) journalist
(B) author
(C) anchor
(D) private investigator

18. Taking up this job might mean giving up on _______________
(A) junk food
(B) watching TV
(C) weekends
(D) hanging out with friends

19. What are two essential skills for this job?
(A) reading and writing
(B) driving and cooking
(C) singing and dancing
(D) communication and listening

20. What are the qualifications required for this job?
(A) Journalism and Mass comm.
(B) Masters degree in Physics
(C) Bachelor of Science
(D) Engineering

21. What is the duration of the course?
(A) a week
(B) a month
(C) two weeks
(D) three weeks

22. What is the timing of the class for teenagers?
(A) 4.15 – 5.30 pm
(B) 7.30 – 8 pm
(C) 5.30 – 6.45 pm
(D) 6.00 – 7.15 pm

23. What is the meaning of the word 'agility'?
(A) to be able to move quickly
(B) to be able to sleep better
(C) to be able to fight illnesses
(D) to be very strong

24. What is the duration of the classes?
(A) one hour
(B) one hour and fifteen minutes
(C) two hours
(D) one and the half hour

25. Which of these things can NOT be learned at these classes?
(A) relaxation technique
(B) cooking healthy food
(C) self-discipline
(D) good posture

26. What is the other name for Kolkata that the letter mentions?
(A) City of joy
(B) City of dreams
(C) City of pleasure
(D) City of tourists

27. What kind of a place is Nicco Park?
(A) Planetarium
(B) Museum
(C) Amusement park
(D) Zoological garden

28. How many trees are there at the Botanical Gardens?
   (A) 10,000   (B) 12,000
   (C) 1,200   (D) 1,20,000

29. Which of these animals will not be found in the Alipore Zoo?
   (A) Indian Elephant
   (B) African Lion
   (C) Royal Bengal Tiger
   (D) Emperor Penguin

30. Which of these places in Kolkata has Bikash NOT visited?
   (A) Birla Planetarium
   (B) Victoria Memorial
   (C) Botanical Gardens
   (D) Nicco Park

1.	A B C D	7.	A B C D	13.	A B C D	19	A B C D	25.	A B C D
2.	A B C D	8.	A B C D	14.	A B C D	20.	A B C D	26.	A B C D
3.	A B C D	9.	A B C D	15.	A B C D	21.	A B C D	27.	A B C D
4.	A B C D	10.	A B C D	16.	A B C D	22.	A B C D	28.	A B C D
5.	A B C D	11.	A B C D	17.	A B C D	23.	A B C D	29.	A B C D
6.	A B C D	12.	A B C D	18.	A B C D	24.	A B C D	30.	A B C D

SPOKEN AND WRITTEN EXPRESSION; PUNCTUATION

PRACTICE EXERCISE

Choose the correct option to make appropriate requests, refusals and apologies in the following situations.

1. You are writing an exam. The only pen you carried with you has stopped working. (Request)
   (A) Could I borrow a pen, please?
   (B) Give me your pen.
   (C) Pen please!
   (D) I need a pen.

2. Your teacher accuses you of cheating during the exam. You know you didn't. (Refuse politely)
   (A) I'm sorry, but there has been a misunderstanding.
   (B) No way.
   (C) No but thanks for asking.
   (D) Are you out of your mind?

3. You forgot to return the pen you borrowed from your friend. Now you have lost it. (Apologize)
   (A) I lost your pen.
   (B) I already returned your pen, you must have forgotten.
   (C) I'm so sorry I lost your pen.
   (D) Never mind.

4. You lost your friend's pen. You apologize to him and he readily forgives you. He says _________. (Accept apology)
   (A) Get out of my sight.
   (B) You should be sorry.
   (C) Thanks for losing my pen.
   (D) That's all right.

5. You are in the store and your friend asks you to help steal something. You don't approve. (Refuse strongly)
   (A) Sure.
   (B) Absolutely not.
   (C) I'll think about it.
   (D) Of course.

6. Your car broke down and you need to go to work. You see your neighbour, who goes the same way just starting for work. (Request)
   (A) I'm coming with you.
   (B) Drive fast!
   (C) If you don't mind, could I come with you?
   (D) Let's go!

7. You enter office in a hurry and while walking past someone's desk, you accidentally drop some papers off his desk. (Apologize formally)
   (A) I'm terribly sorry, I should have watched my step.
   (B) Please pick those up.
   (C) You were on my way.
   (D) I'm in a rush.

8. You are a restaurant manager. A guest is smoking inside the restaurant and he is not supposed to. While asking him to stop you must make sure he is not offended. (Request, formal)

(A) Stop smoking immediately!
(B) If you don't mind Sir, could you please stop smoking?
(C) If you don't mind Sir, could you leave?
(D) Don't you know Sir you are not supposed to smoke here?

9. You were playing with your brother's favourite toy and you broke it. (Apologize informally)
(A) Not that you paid for it.
(B) You gave me a broken toy.
(C) I'll get you a new toy.
(D) I'm sorry I wasn't careful.

10. A friend invites you to a party. You can't make it. (Refuse politely)
(A) No way!
(B) Absolutely not!
(C) No, but thanks for inviting me.
(D) Please don't invite me.

11. You have guests over. They love the desert you made. You want to offer them a second helping. (Request)
(A) Serve yourselves.
(B) Please help yourselves.
(C) The cake's on the table.
(D) Would you like some more cake?

12. You were angry and you called someone a name. You realize your fault later. (Apologize)
(A) I shouldn't have said that.
(B) You deserve it.
(C) I can't control my anger.
(D) Calm down.

13. A neighbour who is going on a vacation asks you to feed his dog. You cannot do this. (Refuse politely)
(A) I hate dogs.
(B) I'm afraid it won't be possible.
(C) Leave me alone.
(D) Never!

14. A friend wants to copy your homework. You worked hard on it and do not like the idea. (Strong refusal)
(A) I'd rather you didn't.
(B) Sure.
(C) No chance.
(D) Go ahead!

15. You are leaving office in a hurry so that you don't miss your doctor's appointment. A colleague wants to talk. (Refuse politely)
(A) Get out of my way.
(B) I'm afraid I have to leave.
(C) What's up?
(D) No, I don't want to talk.

II. **Choose the correct option to join the following sentences.**

16. We may have to take the airplane. Train tickets are not available.
(A) since   (B) but
(C) and   (D) so

17. You treated him badly. He is doing the same to you.
(A) since   (B) but
(C) and   (D) so

18. He is not feeling well. He refuses to take rest.
(A) yet   (B) until
(C) and   (D) so

19. He cannot afford to pay his fees. He is poor.
(A) if   (B) as
(C) and   (D) so

20. He contributed to the charity regularly. He was not rich.
(A) since   (B) as
(C) and   (D) although

21. Men may come or go. We are here forever.
(A) since   (B) but
(C) and   (D) so

22. Apologize to the whole class. You will be expelled.
(A) since   (B) but
(C) Otherwise   (D) so

23. Nobody opened the door. He went away.
(A) and   (B) so
(C) for   (D) but

24. You promised to work hard. You continue to be lazy.
(A) not   (B) or
(C) yet   (D) so

25. Maya failed her test. She made many silly mistakes.
(A) and   (B) or
(C) yet   (D) because

I. Choose the correct option which contains the pair(s) of clauses that can be connected with a semi-colon.

26. (A) I hate rice pudding dairy products don't agree with me.
    (B) Spain is lovely hot weather and friendly people.
    (C) Spain lovely beaches, endless blue sea and great weather.
    (D) Spain is a lovely country the beaches are endless and the weather is always good.

27. (A) Paris is a beautiful city wide streets and sunshine.
    (B) Havana is a lovely city rice pudding is one of my favourite foods.
    (C) I would love to go to France Paris is a lovely city.
    (D) I would love to go to Greece I love ancient history.

28. (A) Understanding grammar is very important despite its complexity.
    (B) Understanding grammar is very important clear communication is an essential skill.
    (C) Understanding grammar is very important most high level jobs require good writing skills.
    (D) Understanding grammar is very important although it is not always the most fascinating subject on the planet.

29. Which can/should be connected with a semi-colon?
    (A) The stock exchange fell sharply investor confidence is very low.
    (B) The stock exchange fell sharply many investors decided to sell their shares.
    (C) The stock exchange fell sharply a difficult day for everybody.
    (D) The stock exchange fell sharply I would wait before selling your shares.

30. (A) I'm not going on holiday this year I am very short of money.
    (B) I'm not going on holiday this year no time!!
    (C) I'm not going on holiday this year too expensive!
    (D) I'm not going on holiday this year hot weather doesn't agree with me.

—Darken Your Choice with HB Pencil—

1.	Ⓐ Ⓑ Ⓒ Ⓓ	7.	Ⓐ Ⓑ Ⓒ Ⓓ	13.	Ⓐ Ⓑ Ⓒ Ⓓ	19	Ⓐ Ⓑ Ⓒ Ⓓ	25.	Ⓐ Ⓑ Ⓒ Ⓓ
2.	Ⓐ Ⓑ Ⓒ Ⓓ	8.	Ⓐ Ⓑ Ⓒ Ⓓ	14.	Ⓐ Ⓑ Ⓒ Ⓓ	20.	Ⓐ Ⓑ Ⓒ Ⓓ	26.	Ⓐ Ⓑ Ⓒ Ⓓ
3.	Ⓐ Ⓑ Ⓒ Ⓓ	9.	Ⓐ Ⓑ Ⓒ Ⓓ	15.	Ⓐ Ⓑ Ⓒ Ⓓ	21.	Ⓐ Ⓑ Ⓒ Ⓓ	27.	Ⓐ Ⓑ Ⓒ Ⓓ
4.	Ⓐ Ⓑ Ⓒ Ⓓ	10.	Ⓐ Ⓑ Ⓒ Ⓓ	16.	Ⓐ Ⓑ Ⓒ Ⓓ	22.	Ⓐ Ⓑ Ⓒ Ⓓ	28.	Ⓐ Ⓑ Ⓒ Ⓓ
5.	Ⓐ Ⓑ Ⓒ Ⓓ	11.	Ⓐ Ⓑ Ⓒ Ⓓ	17.	Ⓐ Ⓑ Ⓒ Ⓓ	23.	Ⓐ Ⓑ Ⓒ Ⓓ	29.	Ⓐ Ⓑ Ⓒ Ⓓ
6.	Ⓐ Ⓑ Ⓒ Ⓓ	12.	Ⓐ Ⓑ Ⓒ Ⓓ	18.	Ⓐ Ⓑ Ⓒ Ⓓ	24.	Ⓐ Ⓑ Ⓒ Ⓓ	30.	Ⓐ Ⓑ Ⓒ Ⓓ

MODEL TEST PAPER

PRACTICE EXERCISE

SECTION-I : WORD AND STRUCTURE KNOWLEDGE

Choose the best word/phrase to complete each sentence.

1. This train is the only link __________ the village and the city.
   (A) from (B) for
   (C) between (D) to

2. If you don't know the meaning of a word, you can look it __________ in a dictionary.
   (A) for (B) up
   (C) down (D) to

3. He was __________ that he had failed his driving test.
   (A) Devastated (B) deviated
   (C) disgusted (D) derailed

4. If you act in haste, everything will go to waste. The word haste means __________.
   (A) Alone (B) selfishly
   (C) slowly (D) a hurry

5. He's had several arguments with his boss. The word argument can be replaced by _______.
   (A) fire ins (B) run ins
   (C) talk back (D) back into

6. People still have __________ doubts about his fitness.
   (A) __ (B) much
   (C) lot of (D) any

7. We don't know what happened. We can only __________ on it.
   (A) Expect
   (B) detect
   (C) guesswork
   (D) speculate

8. I'm going to attend the talk by the noted economist Amartya Sen. 'Noted' means __________.
   (A) Famous
   (B) strict
   (C) intelligent
   (D) controversial

9. If I were a tiger, I __________ scare away all the people.
   (A) have to
   (B) would like to
   (C) like to
   (D) could able to

Choose the appropriate idiom.

10. He's doesn't like playing outdoors, he's an absolute __________.
    (A) couch head
    (B) sleepy head
    (C) bookworm
    (D) lazy tom

11. When he scored top marks, he was __________.
    (A) jumped out of his skin
    (B) on cloud and stars
    (C) high on joy
    (D) over the moon

Find where the error is in the sentence.

12. She walk | all the way | to school | everyday.
    (A) | (B) | (C) | (D)

13. We can't | reach school | lately or we | will be punished.
    (A) | (B) | (C) | (D)

14. The lady | within the black coat | is not | our headmistress.
    (A) | (B) | (C) | (D)

15. He studied | really hard | and performed really | goodly in the test.
    (A) | (B) | (C) | (D)

Choose the best option to complete each sentence.

16. The thief ___________ through a hole in the fence to enter the garden.
    (A) crept   (B) bunged
    (C) swept   (D) crowed

17. A large ________ of whales was following the ship.
    (A) group   (B) class
    (C) school   (D) flock

18. We ________ completed all the remaining work for the school day.
    (A) have just   (B) had just
    (C) have just been   (D) had just been

19. The man had a nasty ________ running from his forehead to his cheek.
    (A) Mole   (B) scar
    (C) tear   (D) beard

20. He ________ his hands in several places as he fell.
    (A) pain   (B) ache
    (C) sore   (D) cut

Match the following sentences with the words below.

21. "Do you think you could type this out for me?" ________ ___________.

22. "Men at work – take diversion." ________________.

23. "Power switches – keep away." ________ ________.

24. "Let's go to the beach." ________ ________.

(a) A suggestion
(b) A request
(c) An announcement
(d) An order

Choose the word that doesn't belong.

25. salad, ketchup, smoothie, custard
    (A) salad   (B) ketchup
    (C) smoothie   (D) custard

26. hop, sway, skip, jump
    (A) hop   (B) sway
    (C) skip   (D) jump

CHOOSE THE CORRECT ANSWER.

27. The senior ________ of this restaurant keeps all his recipes secret.
    (A) cooker   (B) cookie
    (C) chef   (D) chief

28. In India it is ____________ to greet visitors with a Namaste.
    (A) customary   (B) ordinary
    (C) honorary   (D) preliminary

29. Limousines, casinos, yachts; he really lives his life ______________.
    (A) on the high-flyer
    (B) a real casanova
    (C) in the fast lane
    (D) full of gizmos

30. Vinod ____________ finish the race though he was tired.
    (A) could able to   (B) didn't able to
    (C) managed to   (D) was possible to

Read the passage and answer the questions that follow.

For some time now, I have been trying to decide who makes the world's best icecream. I have narrowed my list down to four manufacturers: Bobbins Naturals, Wall's, Wunderburst or Marshal. Let's start with Bobbins. They make very good ice cream. They have lots and lots of yummy flavours, but that's really not important - because I always get coffee flavour. They make the best coffee ice cream in the world. I've never drunk real hot coffee, but people tell me that Bobbins' coffee ice cream tastes just like the real thing. Besides, Bobbins uses all natural ingredients to make their ice cream which is a really good idea.

Second, there is Wall's. Wall's makes excellent ice cream. Like Bobbins, Wall's uses natural ingredients. But they only make three different flavours — strawberry, vanilla and choconut — but they make them really creamy and fruity. Especially the strawberry. Every bite of it reminds me of the strawberries that I used to eat at my gran's house. The vanilla flavour is wonderful. It is very smooth and has a fresh, creamy flavour. But the choconut flavour is the best. It is made with real cocoa beans from Columbia. I didn't know where Columbia is, so I looked for it on a map. I discovered that it is in South America! That's a long way to go to get cocoa, so it must be good. I would say that the only drawback to Wall's ice cream is that they only make three different flavours. Third, we have Wunderburst. Wunderburst ice cream is okay. They don't have many good flavours. Actually, the only Wunderburst flavour I like is Caramel. It is vanilla with little chunks of toffee in it. As you eat the ice cream, you can crunch through the toffee. That's pretty fun.

Finally, there is Marshal. Marshal ice cream is mediocre. The only good thing about Marshal is that it is relatively inexpensive. You can buy a whole carton of Marsha Ice cream for ₹ 50.00. That's only my two - week allowance.

31. Which of the following would be the best title for this passage?
    (A) Strawberry, Vanilla, Choconut, and Toffee
    (B) The Four Top Ice Cream Manufacturers
    (C) The Finest Ice Cream in the World
    (D) Picking the Best Ice Cream Manufacturer

32. If the author wanted to get some coffee ice cream, where would he or she probably go?
    (A) Wunderburst
    (B) Bobbins
    (C) Marshal
    (D) Wall's

33. According to the passage, the author likes Bobbins ice cream because it _________.
    (A) is all natural
    (B) is made in Columbia
    (C) comes in toffee flavour
    (D) is mediocre

34. The author writes, "That's a long way to go to get cocoa, so it must be good." Using this information, we can understand that the author believes that _________.
    (A) Wall's is spending a lot of money on its ingredients
    (B) Columbia makes the best cocoa in the world
    (C) things that are hard to get must be high quality
    (D) cocoa from the other parts of the world is not very good

35. The author likes Wunderburst ice cream because it _______.
    (A) is relatively inexpensive
    (B) has toffee in it
    (C) is made in Columbia
    (D) is okay

36. According to the passage, how is Bobbins ice cream different from Wall's?
   (1) Bobbins has many different flavours and Wall's does not.
   (2) Bobbins uses all natural ingredients and Wall's does not.
   (3) Bobbins is very expensive and Wall's is not.
   (A) 1 only
   (B) 1 and 2 only
   (C) 2 and 3 only
   (D) 1, 2 and 3

37. Given the information in the passage, which of the following statements would the author mostlikely agree with?
   (A) Each manufacturer has its strengths and weaknesses.
   (B) The best manufacturers are the ones with the most flavours.
   (C) Manufacturers with fewer flavours are not usually popular.
   (D) Each manufacturer is good for different reasons.

Read the following list and answer the questions that follow.
➤ They bring you the menu and then become rare to find.
➤ They give you stale bread you didn't ask for and then charge you for it.
➤ They ignore you when you try to catch their eye.
➤ They give you mineral water when you want tap water and you pay throughthe nose for it.
➤ They serve you food that's outright bad, and when you want to complain, they look down their noses at you.
➤ They bring you the bill, and take their own time coming to collect the money.
➤ They are not prompt with service but expect a hefty tip.

38. The above list is 'The top complaints about ____________.'
   (A) chefs   (B) servers
   (C) waiters   (D) customers

39. How is the bread that they give you?
   (A) Moist   (B) Fresh
   (C) Soft   (D) Old

40. According to this list, though they are lethargic to serve you, they expect a _____ reward.
   (A) Small   (B) reasonable
   (C) big   (D) little

41. They bring you the menu and then ________________.
   (A) Disappear   (B) go back stage
   (C) evaporate   (D) camouflage

42. When you want to call them, they ______.
   (A) smile at you
   (B) wave out to you
   (C) pretend not to notice
   (D) come over immediately

43. When you say something is badly prepared, they ________.
   (A) don't listen to you
   (B) blow their noses at you
   (C) start crying and sniffing
   (D) treat you as if you were inferior

44. The water they give you is ________.
   (A) Smelly   (B) scented
   (C) expensive   (D) cheap

SECTION-III : SPOKEN AND WRITTEN EXPRESSION

Choose the best option for each situation.

45. Sheila:____________________________
   Tina : Oh, I stayed at home and watched TV.
   (A) How was work yesterday?
   (B) What did you do all weekend?
   (C) Did you enjoy the beach?
   (D) Have you been sick?

46. Visitor : Can you tell me how to get to the bank, please?
   Policeman: ____________________________

(A) Go away, don't bother me now.

(B) Turn left at the next traffic lights.

(C) Where are you from?

(D) It's to the north cast.

Choose the best option to complete the conversation from the options below.

Jim : Hi, Tara, _________ (47) _________ you're free tomorrow night.

Tara : I guess I am. _________ (48) _________

Jim : I've just got a couple of tickets for the new Dark Knight movie. Are you interested?

Tara : Definitely, _________ (49) _________.

Jim : _________ (50) _________. See you tomorrow then.

47. (A) Can you tell

(B) I was wondering if

(C) Will you be

(D) Do you think if

48. (A) Why do you ask?

(B) What's your problem?

(C) I'm not sure.

(D) Sorry, I'm not.

49. (A) Not this tim.

(B) Thanks for inviting me.

(C) I'm coming.

(D) Sorry to disappoint you.

50. (A) No problem.

(B) Not an issue.

(C) Not again.

(D) No hassles.

—Darken Your Choice with HB Pencil—

1.	Ⓐ	Ⓑ	Ⓒ	Ⓓ	11.	Ⓐ	Ⓑ	Ⓒ	Ⓓ	21.	Ⓐ	Ⓑ	Ⓒ	Ⓓ	31.	Ⓐ	Ⓑ	Ⓒ	Ⓓ	41.	Ⓐ	Ⓑ	Ⓒ	Ⓓ
2.	Ⓐ	Ⓑ	Ⓒ	Ⓓ	12.	Ⓐ	Ⓑ	Ⓒ	Ⓓ	22.	Ⓐ	Ⓑ	Ⓒ	Ⓓ	32.	Ⓐ	Ⓑ	Ⓒ	Ⓓ	42.	Ⓐ	Ⓑ	Ⓒ	Ⓓ
3.	Ⓐ	Ⓑ	Ⓒ	Ⓓ	13.	Ⓐ	Ⓑ	Ⓒ	Ⓓ	23.	Ⓐ	Ⓑ	Ⓒ	Ⓓ	33.	Ⓐ	Ⓑ	Ⓒ	Ⓓ	43.	Ⓐ	Ⓑ	Ⓒ	Ⓓ
4.	Ⓐ	Ⓑ	Ⓒ	Ⓓ	14.	Ⓐ	Ⓑ	Ⓒ	Ⓓ	24.	Ⓐ	Ⓑ	Ⓒ	Ⓓ	34.	Ⓐ	Ⓑ	Ⓒ	Ⓓ	44.	Ⓐ	Ⓑ	Ⓒ	Ⓓ
5.	Ⓐ	Ⓑ	Ⓒ	Ⓓ	15.	Ⓐ	Ⓑ	Ⓒ	Ⓓ	25.	Ⓐ	Ⓑ	Ⓒ	Ⓓ	35.	Ⓐ	Ⓑ	Ⓒ	Ⓓ	45.	Ⓐ	Ⓑ	Ⓒ	Ⓓ
6.	Ⓐ	Ⓑ	Ⓒ	Ⓓ	16.	Ⓐ	Ⓑ	Ⓒ	Ⓓ	26.	Ⓐ	Ⓑ	Ⓒ	Ⓓ	36.	Ⓐ	Ⓑ	Ⓒ	Ⓓ	46.	Ⓐ	Ⓑ	Ⓒ	Ⓓ
7.	Ⓐ	Ⓑ	Ⓒ	Ⓓ	17.	Ⓐ	Ⓑ	Ⓒ	Ⓓ	27.	Ⓐ	Ⓑ	Ⓒ	Ⓓ	37.	Ⓐ	Ⓑ	Ⓒ	Ⓓ	47.	Ⓐ	Ⓑ	Ⓒ	Ⓓ
8.	Ⓐ	Ⓑ	Ⓒ	Ⓓ	18.	Ⓐ	Ⓑ	Ⓒ	Ⓓ	28.	Ⓐ	Ⓑ	Ⓒ	Ⓓ	38.	Ⓐ	Ⓑ	Ⓒ	Ⓓ	48.	Ⓐ	Ⓑ	Ⓒ	Ⓓ
9.	Ⓐ	Ⓑ	Ⓒ	Ⓓ	19.	Ⓐ	Ⓑ	Ⓒ	Ⓓ	29.	Ⓐ	Ⓑ	Ⓒ	Ⓓ	39.	Ⓐ	Ⓑ	Ⓒ	Ⓓ	49.	Ⓐ	Ⓑ	Ⓒ	Ⓓ
10.	Ⓐ	Ⓑ	Ⓒ	Ⓓ	20.	Ⓐ	Ⓑ	Ⓒ	Ⓓ	30.	Ⓐ	Ⓑ	Ⓒ	Ⓓ	40.	Ⓐ	Ⓑ	Ⓒ	Ⓓ	50.	Ⓐ	Ⓑ	Ⓒ	Ⓓ

HINTS AND SOLUTIONS

1. SYNONYMS, ANTONYMS, HOMOPHONES AND HOMONYMS

Answer Key

I									
1. (A)	2. (B)	3. (D)	4. (C)	5. (A)	6. (B)	7. (A)	8. (B)	9. (B)	10. (C)
11. (C)	12. (C)	13. (A)	14. (D)	15. (C)	16. (A)	17. (B)	18. (C)	19. (C)	20. (C)

II									
21. (A)	22. (C)	23. (B)	24. (D)	25. (B)					

HOTS (ACHIEVERS SECTION)

26. (A)	27. (D)	28. (B)	29. (C)	30. (A)

2. SPELLINGS AND COLLOCATION

Answer Key

I									
1. (B)	2. (D)	3. (C)	4. (B)	5. (C)					

II									
6. (A)	7. (C)	8. (B)	9. (D)	10. (C)	11. (B)	12. (D)	13. (C)		

II									
14. (A)	15. (B)	16. (C)	17. (B)	18. (A)	19. (A)	20. (A)	21. (A)	22. (A)	23. (B)
24. (A)	25. (C)								

HOTS (ACHIEVERS SECTION)

I				
26. (A)	27. (B)	28. (C)		

II				
29. (D)	30. (B)			

Answer Key

1. (B)	2. (A)	3. (D)	4. (C)	5. (B)	6. (A)	7. (C)	8. (B)	9. (D)	10. (C)
11. (A)	12. (C)	13. (D)	14. (D)	15. (A)	16. (C)	17. (B)	18. (D)	19. (D)	20. (B)

HOTS (ACHIEVERS SECTION)

21. (A)	22. (C)	23. (D)	24. (A)	25. (B)

4. PHRASAL VERBS AND IDIOMS, MODALS, WORD ORDER

Answer Key

I									
1. (D)	2. (D)	3. (B)	4. (A)	5. (A)	6. (D)	7. (B)	8. (A)	9. (B)	10. (B)
11. (D)	12. (A)	13. (B)	14. (D)	15. (B)	16. (A)	17. (C)	18. (C)	19. (C)	20. (A)
II									
21. (C)	22. (B)	23. (B)	24. (D)	25. (A)					

HOTS (ACHIEVERS SECTION)

I			
26. (A)	27. (A)	28. (B)	29. (C)
II			
30. (B)			

5. NOUNS AND PRONOUNS

Answer Key

I									
1. (D)	2. (A)	3. (D)	4. (B)	5. (A)	6. (C)	7. (B)	8. (B)	9. (C)	10. (A)
II									
11. (A)	12. (D)	13. (C)	14. (A)	15. (B)	16. (C)	17. (D)	18. (A)	19. (B)	20. (C)
II									
21. (A)	22. (D)	23. (B)	24. (C)	25. (B)					

HOTS (ACHIEVERS SECTION)				
26. (A)	27. (B)	28. (B)	29. (A)	30. (B)

6. VERBS AND ADVERBS

Answer Key

I									
1. (A)	2. (B)	3. (C)	4. (D)	5. (B)	6. (D)	7. (C)	8. (A)	9. (B)	10. (A)
11. (B)	12. (D)	13. (A)	14. (B)	15. (C)					

II									
16. (A)	17. (C)	18. (D)	19. (A)	20. (A)	21. (A)	22. (B)	23. (A)	24. (C)	25. (C)

HOTS (ACHIEVERS SECTION)

I			
26. (C)	27. (B)	28. (A)	

II			
29. (B)	30. (D)		

7. ADJECTIVES

Answer Key

I									
1. (A)	2. (C)	3. (A)	4. (C)	5. (B)	6. (C)	7. (B)	8. (A)	9. (C)	10. (C)

II									
11. (C)	12. (A)	13. (C)	14. (C)	15. (B)	16. (A)	17. (B)	18. (C)	19. (B)	20. (B)
21. (C)	22. (C)	23. (A)	24. (B)	25. (C)					

HOTS (ACHIEVERS SECTION)

26. (B)	27. (C)	28. (C)	29. (B)	30. (D)

Answer Key

1. (A)	2. (D)	3. (B)	4. (A)	5. (B)	6. (B)	7. (B)	8. (D)	9. (A)	10. (C)
11. (C)	12. (A)	13. (C)	14. (C)	15. (D)	16. (D)	17. (C)	18. (B)	19. (C)	20. (B)
21. (A)	22. (D)	23. (D)	24. (D)	25. (A)					

HOTS (ACHIEVERS SECTION)

26. (A)	27. (B)	28. (B)	29. (C)	30. (B)

9. CONJUNCTIONS AND TENSES

Answer Key

I									
1. (A)	2. (D)	3. (B)	4. (C)	5. (A)	6. (D)	7. (A)	8. (B)	9. (A)	10. (D)

II									
11. (A)	12. (B)	13. (B)	14. (C)	15. (A)	16. (C)	17. (C)	18. (C)	19. (D)	20. (D)
21. (C)	22. (B)	23. (B)	24. (C)	25. (B)					

HOTS (ACHIEVERS SECTION)

26. (A)	27. (A)	28. (A)	29. (C)	30. (C)

10. VOICES AND NARRATION

Answer Key

1. (C)	2. (B)	3. (A)	4. (C)	5. (B)	6. (C)	7. (D)	8. (B)	9. (B)	10. (B)
11. (A)	12. (B)	13. (C)	14. (D)	15. (B)	16. (B)	17. (B)	18. (D)	19. (B)	20. (D)
21. (A)	22. (A)	23. (A)	24. (B)	25. (C)					

HOTS (ACHIEVERS SECTION)

26. (D)	27. (D)	28. (D)	29. (D)	30. (D)

11. VOCABULARY

Answer Key

I

1. (A)	2. (C)	3. (B)	4. (D)	5. (A)	6. (B)	7. (D)	8. (C)	9. (A)	10. (B)

II

11. (A)	12. (C)	13. (B)	14. (D)	15. (A)	16. (C)	17. (A)	18. (B)	19. (D)	20. (B)

II

21. (C)	22. (B)	23. (A)	24. (D)	25. (B)					

HOTS (ACHIEVERS SECTION)

26. (C)	27. (B)	28. (A)	29. (D)	30. (B)

12. SEQUENCING-STORIES, EVENTS AND SNIPPETS

Answer Key

1. (B)	2. (B)	3. (A)	4. (A)	5. (A)	6. (B)	7. (B)	8. (D)	9. (C)	10. (B)
11. (A)	12. (C)	13. (B)	14. (C)	15. (D)	16. (B)	17. (D)	18. (C)	19. (A)	20. (B)

HOTS (ACHIEVERS SECTION)

21. (D)	22. (B)	23. (A)	24. (B)	25. (D)

13. COMPREHENSION

Answer Key

1. (B)	2. (A)	3. (D)	4. (C)	5. (A)	6. (C)	7. (A)	8. (B)	9. (D)	10. (D)
11. (A)	12. (D)	13. (B)	14. (B)	15. (A)	16. (B)	17. (C)	18. (C)	19. (D)	20. (A)
21. (B)	22. (D)	23. (A)	24. (B)	25. (B)	26. (A)	27. (C)	28. (B)	29. (D)	30. (B)

Answer Key

I									
1. (A)	2. (A)	3. (C)	4. (D)	5. (B)	6. (C)	7. (A)	8. (B)	9. (D)	10. (C)
11. (D)	12. (A)	13. (B)	14. (C)	15. (B)					

II									
16. (A)	17. (D)	18. (A)	19. (B)	20. (D)	21. (B)	22. (C)	23. (B)	24. (C)	25. (D)

HOTS (ACHIEVERS SECTION)

26. (D)	27. (D)	28. (B)	29. (B)	30. (D)

MODEL TEST PAPER

Answer Key

1. (C)	2. (B)	3. (A)	4. (D)	5. (C)	6. (A)	7. (D)	8. (A)	9. (B)	10. (C)
11. (D)	12. (A)	13. (C)	14. (B)	15. (D)	16. (A)	17. (C)	18. (A)	19. (B)	20. (D)
21. (B)	22. (C)	23. (D)	24. (A)	25. (A)	26. (B)	27. (C)	28. (A)	29. (C)	30. (C)
31. (B)	32. (B)	33. (A)	34. (B)	35. (A)	36. (A)	37. (D)	38. (C)	39. (D)	40. (C)
41. (A)	42. (C)	43. (D)	44. (C)	45. (B)	46. (B)	47. (B)	48. (A)	49. (B)	50. (A)

SAMPLE OMR ANSWER SHEET

1. STUDENT NAME (IN ENGLISH CAPITAL LETTERS ONLY)

Students must write and darken the respective circles completely using HB Pencil only. Othewise their Answer Sheets will not be evaluated.

PERSONAL DETAILS

2. SCHOOL CODE

3. CLASS

4. SECTION

5. ROLL NO.

6. QUESTION PAPER SET

A ○
B ○
C ○
D ○

7. MOBILE NUMBER

8. GENDER

MALE ○
FEMALE ○

9. STREAM

(Only for Class XI and XII Students)

MATHEMATICS ○
BIOLOGY ○
OTHERS ○

MARK YOUR ANSWERS

1. (A) (B) (C) (D) 26. (A) (B) (C) (D)
2. (A) (B) (C) (D) 27. (A) (B) (C) (D)
3. (A) (B) (C) (D) 28. (A) (B) (C) (D)
4. (A) (B) (C) (D) 29. (A) (B) (C) (D)
5. (A) (B) (C) (D) 30. (A) (B) (C) (D)
6. (A) (B) (C) (D) 31. (A) (B) (C) (D)
7. (A) (B) (C) (D) 32. (A) (B) (C) (D)
8. (A) (B) (C) (D) 33. (A) (B) (C) (D)
9. (A) (B) (C) (D) 34. (A) (B) (C) (D)
10. (A) (B) (C) (D) 35. (A) (B) (C) (D)
11. (A) (B) (C) (D) 36. (A) (B) (C) (D)
12. (A) (B) (C) (D) 37. (A) (B) (C) (D)
13. (A) (B) (C) (D) 38. (A) (B) (C) (D)
14. (A) (B) (C) (D) 39. (A) (B) (C) (D)
15. (A) (B) (C) (D) 40. (A) (B) (C) (D)
16. (A) (B) (C) (D) 41. (A) (B) (C) (D)
17. (A) (B) (C) (D) 42. (A) (B) (C) (D)
18. (A) (B) (C) (D) 43. (A) (B) (C) (D)
19. (A) (B) (C) (D) 44. (A) (B) (C) (D)
20. (A) (B) (C) (D) 45. (A) (B) (C) (D)
21. (A) (B) (C) (D) 46. (A) (B) (C) (D)
22. (A) (B) (C) (D) 47. (A) (B) (C) (D)
23. (A) (B) (C) (D) 48. (A) (B) (C) (D)
24. (A) (B) (C) (D) 49. (A) (B) (C) (D)
25. (A) (B) (C) (D) 50. (A) (B) (C) (D)

Signature of the Student & Date of Examination

Signature of the Invigilator & Date of Examination